What if I TELL?

GINA McCABE

WHAT IF I TELL

Published by Winding Road Books

ISBN 978-0-9815139-0-4

6168583   12/08

M   B & T

                  14.95

Copyright © 2008 by Gina McCabe

All Rights Reserved

Printed in the United States of America

March 2008

First Edition

www.windingroadbooks.com

To anyone who does anything
to stop the stigma and silence

MACDONALD PUBLIC LIBRARY

Winding Road Books

I was only six and already an expert at hiding things; that was normal for me. I put together my favorite outfit: the gray sweater and stretchy navy polyester overalls, matched proudly with my new Montreal Expos cap. I tucked my straggly blonde hair up into the hat the best I knew how and darted out the front door. There were still remnants of a homemade banana muffin with peanut butter on my face, and I hadn't bothered brushing my teeth.

"Bye, mom," I hollered, sneaking down the front steps without letting her see what I was wearing. I didn't wait for my brother, Mike, either. I just ran.

It's picture day. I don't want to wear a dress!

Our prim and proper suburban Montreal home, a 1960s brick rambler at 107 Dorset, was right across the street from Dorset Elementary, the only school in Baie d'Urfe.

At 11:25 a.m., my Kindergarten classmates and I were lined up against the gym doors, fidgeting.

Oh no, I'm next.

Getting dolled up, fixing my hair, and having people gawk at and scrutinize me has always been unbearable.

"You're leaving the cap on?" asked the photographer.

"Yes," I said hopefully.

He looks friendly. Please, please, sir, don't make me take it off.

He showed me a mirror and gave me the opportunity to make any last minute touch-ups. I tried awkwardly to tuck my hair frizzes in a little better and then handed him back the mirror with confidence.

Yes! He's letting me keep it on!

He asked me if I loved the Expos, and I smiled big. I mean, big. The flash snapped. I was so proud of myself.

I didn't have to dress up and look all perfect!

Walking home, I fixated on the asphalt cracks left behind by the harsh Canadian winters. I stepped on every crevice in the road, first with my right foot, then my left. Then I stepped back and switched the order.

Sometimes the cracks were far away, too far to reach with one step, and that irritated me. I had to figure out which ones were too far and which ones were within my range.

Darn it. I keep going sideways. Home is over that way! If I step on every crack, I'll never get there. I have to pick and focus on only the ones that matter. This is so tiring. And it's stupid!

I looked around and made sure no one was watching me execute my ridiculous habits with such intensity.

I kept walking and looked up to the sky in an attempt to ignore the cracks, but I could still feel them under my shoes.

I better start over and pay attention this time.

I backed up across the street and re-did all of my steps.

Step on a crack, and break your mama's back. Don't say that! I don't believe that. I can prove it's not true. See? Crack. There, I did it, and when I get home, everybody will be fine. Everyone will be fine. Everyone. Everybody. Ev. Every. Everyone. Every one. Vuh. Evuh. Evuhreey-one.

I flung the door open, kicked off my navy and white Adidas and ran to my room. I punched myself in the stomach a few times and then beat myself on the head with my wrists. Not too hard, but just enough to feel a bit of pain, tensing up my core and jabbing with the side of my fist and then the bottom of my palm. And I hit equally on both sides, alternating, ten times.

I didn't hear Mlke come in. He ran up behind me, grabbed my hands and pretended to help me punch myself.

"Gina, why are you hitting yourself again?" he asked, laughing hysterically and teasing.

"Shut up," I said, embarrassed. I knew he wasn't trying to be mean, but still.

I pretended that I hadn't been doing anything and started to reach for my toys.

"Leave me alone, Mike" I said. And he bailed, still snickering.

As soon as he left, I let it out like dumping a five gallon bucket.

Thank goodness I'm alone. I feel so nervous.

I picked up my yellow and orange Barbie sports car, and first I grabbed it with my left hand, then put it down and repeated with my right, trying to achieve a perfectly parallel grip and feeling. I accidentally brushed against the dresser with my elbow on the right side, so I had to repeat the sequence again, carefully starting with the right side first this time. Over and over I practiced, until both the left and right activities were executed equally, with precisely the same sensation.

Okay, that's enough. That was good enough. Stop it. Just play!

I sat on my yellow bedspread to play with my
collection of mini perfumes and bit my nails until they were as
short as I could get them. The special nail polish that the
doctor had given me didn't stop me from biting. In fact, it was
disgusting and tasted good. My left pinky and thumb were
bleeding a bit.

Ouch. Man, that stings.

It hurt, but the biting and ripping was so satisfying.
The piece of fingernail that came off fit right between my
lower front teeth, and I could slide it through again and again.

I hit my hip bones with my wrists, five times on each
side, then banged the side of my head on the headboard a
little, then switched sides and switched order, and I made my
way slowly around the room, repeating. I stretched my eyes as
wide as they would go and then shut them tightly, blinking
once to finish off that routine.

*Stretch your eyes. Stretch your hands. Make it hurt. It
feels better when it hurts. Do it again. Get it out.*

Out in the hall, I quietly hit my elbows on the antique
desk. The rounded carvings felt good. As I approached the
long stretch of the hallway, I scratched my fingers down the
walls. It felt awful, especially on my raw fingernails, but I
couldn't resist.

Scratch it. Scratch fast. No one will see you. Do it again. Swipe them both at once. Bend your fingers more so that you'll feel it on your sore nails. Make sure you get your thumbs too. Do it again. Get closer to the wall. Do it harder.

There was nothing to scratch in the living room, and it was too public for any hitting. But the piano was a release, and it was time to practice anyway. I played scales, over and over again, with careful attention to symmetry and perfection. Every key, major and minor, left then right, right then left, then together. It was necessary and tiring, but I knew that the reward of Mrs. Weston's praise during tomorrow afternoon's lesson would be worth the obsession. I played Clementi's Opus 36 twice properly all the way through. Then, I repeated it an octave higher, taking the tempo as fast as I could. That was fun. I did it again, faster and faster. I lost myself in the challenge and the music. I had another piano examination in just a few weeks at the Royal Conservatory of Music in Montreal.

I better do great. Get practicing. I should be practicing more. Every day.

Over dinner I announced confidently with a nervous, teethy smile, "Today was picture day at school!"

"It was not!" my mom laughed, half disapproving. "And, you wore that? Why didn't you tell me, Gina?!"

I just smiled.

I knew you would want me to wear a dress.

Mike chimed in. "Our class pictures aren't until Monday."

"I can't believe this!" mom said.

When the photos came in the mail, the family had a story to tell about how little Gina snuck out of the house so that she could wear her favorite baseball hat in her kindergarten class picture.

It was a nice transition from an earlier event where, as a toddler, in a fit of frustration, I told them I was moving out. I'd packed a suitcase and was standing at our front door.

"Where are you going?" my parents asked.

"I'm moving out and getting an apartment downtown Montreal," I said.

They laughed and asked me how exactly I was planning on paying for this apartment, the food, and so on.

I didn't have any answers, reluctantly admitted that I had it good at home, and decided to stay.

A few months before my eleventh birthday, I finally did get the chance to move away from our Montreal community, and I was elated. My dad received a job offer with a U.S. based consulting firm, and, in the spring of 1981, our family relocated to Cherry Hill, New Jersey.

Elbow Lane was a cul-de-sac filled with other kids our age, and the transition to teenagehood was centered on friends and fun. MTV, playing in bands in our basement, Old Orchard swim team, softball, basketball, field hockey, Rubic's Cube, Atari, Journey, Asia, Loverboy, Izod, Jordache, Ocean Pacific, Docksiders, Pat's Steaks, Slurpees, French braids, and hanging out at our house. I loved our new home and my new friends.

My parents supported us in everything our hearts desired, from music lessons to sports, having friends over, and late nights filled with sneaking around, playing pranks, laughing hysterically and listening to loud music.

My childhood ticks – obsessions with symmetry and pain – disappeared. Instead, my moments alone were spent facing crippling fear.

Every night before going to bed, I checked under and beside my bed and in my closet. Then I would check the guest room, lifting the white hand-knit blanket with embroidered red roses to look under the bed. Obviously, I checked the closet, too, and around the matching white desk and chest of drawers. I didn't check just once. I checked two, three, nine times, depending on how long it took me to fall asleep.

Sometimes it was minutes in between checks, and sometimes it was an hour. It took me long enough just to get the courage to slip out of my bed in the first place, because I was afraid of uncovering myself. And, I was even more apprehensive about stepping onto the carpet and venturing into the dark. Sometimes I took my big math textbook along with me in case I needed a weapon.

It's going to be okay. It's going to be okay. Don't be scared. Do not be scared. Scared.

With my bedside lamp turned on, I'd move slowly, holding my breath and clenching my teeth as I peeked into the dark corners, my heart pounding, my body ready to bolt if I found anything, or anyone. You would have thought I had been kidnapped. I knew logically that no one was there, but I felt a presence and a fear that was so real. I had to check, and I had to do it quietly so that no one would notice.

I shook and trembled, and I believed that the only thing that would help me would be to look in my closet again and make absolutely, positively sure that no one was there. Once I was brave enough to slide the door open, I'd quickly shove the laundry basket and clothes aside, making every bit of the area fully visible. When I thought I saw something, I would rush at it and ram it away with all my force, and "it" usually ended up being a sweatshirt, stuffed animal, or book bag. No one was ever there. But still I checked, and I checked again.

I told myself it was normal to check. It became just another habit. Like stepping on the cracks, I didn't know why I did it, but I just knew that I had to. On nighttime trips to the restroom, I fearfully punched through the shower curtain, to ensure that anyone behind it would be smashed. I would then shove it over to one side, peek carefully around, and slide it over to the opposite side, repeating.

There's no way anyone can be hiding in there now.

Arriving back into my room, I needed to check to ensure that no one had snuck in while I was gone, so I went through the normally scheduled checks, dreading all along that the enemy would appear.

In middle school, I often woke up at 5 a.m. to prepare class readings or homework exercises. Aside from Computer Programming Lab, Chemistry was my favorite subject, partly because I had a huge crush on Mark Mirelli, who sat right behind me, was sweet and cute, had a charming stutter and great taste in music. But I was also obsessed with the periodic table of elements, its memorizable patterns and interrelationships, and mathematical formulas. I fantasized about painting a giant periodic chart on my bedroom wall.

Mark and I became close friends, spent a lot of time listening to Rush and Triumph, and hung out every day with our tight knit group of friends. My best friend Tara and I knew every line to "Sixteen Candles" and "The Outsiders." We listened to Madonna's first album every day after school, and we loved going up to the school to find the guys. There, by the basketball court, we all hung out. True friends, lots of laughs, and loads of fun. Eighth grade was the best year of my youth.

But when I was alone, all of the good went dark. There was a phobia of being chased that I couldn't overcome. Walking home after a sunny day at the pool. On my bike riding home through Old Orchard. Through the back yard after field hockey practice. On a return trip from the Clover shopping center. I was fine one minute, and then, always unexpectedly, came the fear.

Especially when I reached the woods of our back yard. I would be walking toward the house, noticing the trees and leaves, the trails, the hills, and – suddenly – it would kick in. Terror. I could have run forever if I'd needed to. It was a jolt of energy driven by the feeling of being chased. And I would run as fast as I could to get home, looking behind me every twenty seconds. And the feeling lasted as I fiddled with the side door lock and frantically pushed until I was inside. Out of breath and my backpack sliding down my shoulder, I'd slam and lock the door behind me. I used the two seconds between the garage and the laundry room to compose myself before potentially running into my family.

It's scary being a kid. You always feel like someone is going to get you. This is terrible.

As a sophomore, I took walks through those same woods with my boyfriend, Stu, who was a senior at Moorestown. He waited patiently in our living room, watching basketball for an hour or more while I got ready upstairs, obsessing nervously over blemishes, clothes, hair, and makeup.

He and I would often go out for a stroll, venturing all the way through the back of my neighborhood, past the water treatment plant and up to the park at Sharp Elementary. We held hands as we ran across the field to the swings where we'd talk for hours, carve our initials into the dirt and fall in young love.

Stu's recently deceased father had been a pastor. Stu was a self-proclaimed devout Christian who carried on his father's strict opinions. As I got to know him, I realized that he could win a debate on any topic – religion, sports, politics, and a lot of things I didn't even know or care about. He was full of fire and relentless in convincing others to adopt his convictions. I found him intellectually challenging, to the point where he made me question my own beliefs.

Within six months of going out with Stu, I was converted to his standards. I no longer acknowledged my other male friends, and I never went more than an hour without calling him to report everything I'd been doing, including who I'd seen, talked to, and even said hello to. By the end of the school year, I was spending two hours every night on the phone with Stu, explaining myself through bitter tears, apologizing for everything I'd ever done that was not on his list of approved activities. He grilled me about my day and then dove into my past, rehashing everything I'd ever done.

I began to genuinely feel like a bad person for ever having played spin the bottle prior to knowing him. That kind of behavior was like murder in his judgment. The more he criticized me, the more I felt that I needed him, and the more I became disappointed in myself.

I'm so embarrassed about the way he treats me. I hope nobody finds out. Is this really reasonable? I wish I hadn't done all of those bad things so that I wouldn't have to go through all of this. I bet if I died he would feel bad about what he's been doing to me.

The relationship went on for over a year, with promises of future marriage and love everlasting. While Stu harshly condemned my every fault and the small sins of my past, he also pushed my physical boundaries, assuring me that intimacy with him was right and acceptable.

I worked at a women's retail store after school, creating displays and selling business attire. Without giving up any details, I sought advice from my mostly older female co-workers. They didn't have it all together either, but it certainly seemed like they weren't going to bed every night crying and feeling guilty. And, they had friends who were guys. Guys they talked to.

Thanks to Stu going off to college and cheating on me, and me realizing he was a jerk, I eventually got over him as well as his ridiculous judgments. At the same time that I hated how he made me feel, I secretly craved him. But by

junior year, I was back to my outgoing self and glad to be
reunited with real friends who didn't critique me. After all, I
was critical enough of myself that I didn't need anyone else
adding to the list of complaints.

Daytime was a good time. But nighttime was still guilt
and fear. So, I checked, and I checked again. And I prayed for
God's forgiveness and begged Him every night to help me be
a better person.

My last two years of high school were full of parties,
music, and friends. Over the summers I did systems analysis
for the Pennsauken technology firm where my parents both
worked. That was my first exposure to the business world,
including ambitious college students, working lunches, office
politics, and deadlines.

After work, I started to see Paul, who had been asking
me out since before my first date with Stu. Paul was a football
player – tall, strong, and good-looking with a sweet
personality. We went out through my senior prom and the
summer beyond that. Somehow, I missed all the signs that he
had gotten a girl pregnant while we were dating and that he
really wasn't as committed to our relationship as I thought.
We went through our on and off dating cycles, alternately
loving and hurting each other as we went, until eventually we
both gave it up.

When I'd graduated from George Mason University with a degree in English Writing in '93, the Northern Virginia job market had nothing to offer me but entry level or administrative positions. I had been waiting tables throughout college, and despite the long-term benefits of joining a professional organization, I couldn't imagine living on half my current earnings – not to mention the cash I was bringing home.

I considered going to law school and tried court reporting for a year, working mostly on insider trading cases with the Securities and Exchange Commission. I became accustomed to sitting through eight straight hours of depositions where the defendant admitted virtually nothing, and the attorneys, with their Mont Blanc pens, starched shirts and shiny cufflinks, objected to everything. Capturing every manipulated word, I learned how justice is compromised by secrets, alliances, money and personal motives.

These people can't get anything done. No one tells the truth.

Thanks to a friend's recommendation, I ended up landing a temporary position coordinating the CPR program with Fairfax County Fire and Rescue, and my office overlooked their training center's burn building.

As a firefighter, I could help people. But I could never do that. Maybe I should try. There are a few girls in this recruit class. I wonder if I could do it.

I can do it. I'll just work out a lot, talk to the guys who do it and figure out what it takes. I'm going to do it.

It didn't take long to find out that local government hiring was a lengthy process. I continued bartending at Outback in Clifton part-time and eventually received an announcement that Prince William County was recruiting firefighters.

This will be a good excuse for me to get into the best shape of my life.

Following two years' worth of application processes, including a polygraph, physical agility test (which I failed the first time and had to wait another six months to re-take), written exam, interview, and gaining American citizenship, I became one of a dozen career women in the Prince William County Department of Fire and Rescue. In the eighteen weeks

that I spent in recruit school, I learned what it meant to really
work – physically.

While mentally I've always felt that I could learn and
do just about anything with enough training and practice, the
daily physical exertion was all new to me. After ten hour days
of pulling hose lines, throwing ladders, rescuing dummies,
climbing stairs with heavy gear and cutting apart cars, I was
completely worn out and usually asleep by 8 p.m.

Beyond assessing brute requirements, recruit school
tested my self-confidence and pushed me beyond every
imaginable social limit. Daily uniform inspection meant
standing in a line at attention while officers approved the hair
style down to the shoe shine and everything in between. As
part of physical training, our body fat was measured in front of
each other. We paired up in teams of two for sit-ups, ladder
raises, and countless tests and trials. Every activity peeled
back another layer of self-doubt, exposing weaknesses and
uncertainly.

*They're staring at me. I suck at this. I'm not strong
enough. What if I fail? I bet they're talking about me. Do I
look stupid?*

I laughed off the tension with jokes and sarcasm right
up through graduation.

Once recruit school was over, I was assigned to
Engine 4 in Gainesville. I took every opportunity to learn as
much as I could about the fire and rescue service, enrolling in
every training session available, seeking guidance from the
good old boys, and reading training manuals. Elevator rescue,
train rescue, hazardous materials, confined space, vehicle
extrication. I wanted to know it all.

On weekends, I deejayed for extra cash and often
went up to South Jersey to work on music with my brother.
Mike and I shared a passion for music, and we had built a
studio in his home where we wrote and recorded our own
originals, and we re-made hi-NRG dance versions of pop hits.

We were thrilled when our mix of "Don't Speak,"
recorded under the name Clueless, was picked up by ZYX
Records and hit Billboard's Top 10 singles in 1997.
Unfortunately, our high school "friend" who brokered the deal
walked away with the earnings.

Hopeful that we would one day make it in the
industry, we continued recording and tried to get smarter
about the business. Not having the financial means to drop our
jobs and focus only on music, we eventually let the dream
fade. By the time I was twenty-eight, the only performing I did
was singing or playing the piano for personal enjoyment and
at weddings or memorial services.

Within two years in fire and rescue, I had become an Engine driver and a medic. I was promoted to shift work at Engine 16, the first career female to be assigned to a 24-hour unit. I only worked 9 days a month, so two out of every three days, I was at home, launching my own business doing web presence and e-commerce for small and medium-sized companies.

Here I was, a grown working woman – a firefighter – living in my own condo in Manassas, capable and fit, and I still felt the fear. So, I checked. And now it wasn't the guest room and the closet that haunted me. It was the opening to the shared attic. It was the locks on the front door and the access to my fourth floor balcony. It was the sounds I heard outside my window and in the hall, and from the air conditioner or dishwasher. When I was tired, I was terrified. And although no one was there, I knew that at any moment someone could be. In high alert mode, adrenaline pumping, with eyes wide open, I was ready to defend myself. The feeling of fear overtook my body and mind in a nightmare I couldn't escape.

I started to admit to people. "I get so scared at night," I would say. "I'm freakin' terrified."

"Of what?" they would ask.

"I don't know. I'm just afraid that someone is going to break in."

Doug McCabe was the only one I could trust enough to explain my fears in detail. We had been friends since my second year in the Department and had been dating for a couple of years by then. I started to feel more comfortable sharing my fears with him.

He would say things like, "You have nothing to be afraid of" or "no one is going to get you." But it didn't matter. Neither the words nor the logic helped. In fact, if anything, I felt more frustrated and alone because I couldn't get anyone to understand how terrified I really was, including myself. I didn't know why I felt this way; all I knew was that I felt it, that it seemed more real than anything else in my life, and that I hated it.

Finally one afternoon, Doug and I were talking and somehow came to the conclusion that maybe if I kept a gun in my nightstand I would feel safer. I'd learned to shoot a few years before, had been to the range several times, had two rifles of my own for hunting, and thought that a handgun might be a good idea. I had shot a few deer and thought it couldn't be much harder than that.

Doug brought me over a Ruger 9mm KP89 and showed me all of its features. "This one will be perfect for you," he said, "It'll kill anything that comes near you."

We practiced loading and unloading, he showed me how the safety worked – red to green, just like my hunting rifles – and he helped me to outline a plan.

The safety on this thing is tight. But this sure is easier to load than my black powder. No measuring the grains, no packing. Piece of cake. Click and bang. I better hold it tight so that I don't lose control when I shoot it.

"Now, tell me what it is that you think might happen," he said.

"I'm afraid someone is gonna break in and come into my room."

"No one's gonna break in, Gina," he said.

"I know," I replied, "but I can't help that I feel like they will."

"Okay. So keep it right here, okay?"

"Yeah." I turned the gun a little so that I could get to it more easily.

I hope I don't accidentally bust a cap in my sleep or something.

"And if ever someone breaks in, you just shoot 'em."

"Okay, right in the chest?"

He was trying to be serious because he knew how serious I was. "Sure. Give it three shots. Boom, boom, boom," and he motioned one shot right after the other, pointing to his chest.

"But I don't want to see them."

"See what?"

"The person."

"Okay, keep your bedroom door closed and locked. And if someone is there, you just shoot right through the door, here, here and here." He emphasized the different heights. "No matter how short or tall they are, you'll get 'em, babe" he assured me.

"That's a good idea."

For the moment I felt better.

Around 5:30 p.m., Doug headed out for his shift at the public safety communications center.

I'll be okay.

After Letterman, I was tired. I turned off the light and hid myself under the blankets as usual, with just enough open space around my nose to breathe. An hour passed, and I was still wide awake.

Don't try so hard to fall asleep. Just relax and let your mind wander, and you'll fall asleep eventually.

I was starting to feel it. I thought I should check the gun just to make sure it was ready in case I needed it.

I pointed the barrel away from me, and reminded myself to be safe. I practiced cocking it, loading and unloading, turning the safety on and off, and lining it up with the door, just how Doug had said.

I'm not going to need to load or unload it. Just leave it.

I clicked the safety back on and put the gun away.

1:57 a.m., and I was still awake and feeling vulnerable. I turned the television on and took a Tylenol PM.

I should have taken this earlier. Man, I hate when I do this. What's so hard about remembering to take a pill before you go to bed?

Until the Benadryl kicked in, I kept the television on but turned down, so that I could hear if anyone tried to come in. And I sat up like a vigilant until finally I was tired enough to lie down, cover my head with the blankets again, and fall asleep.

A noise woke me up at 4:30 a.m. I darted up, grabbed the gun, flicked the safety off, and pointed. Nothing. I was shaking. My heart was pounding. Nothing. I was trying to breathe quietly so that anyone there wouldn't hear me. I slowly moved down onto the Berber carpet and tried to get a glimpse of the crack underneath my bedroom door. No feet. No shadow. I was scared to breathe. The carpet was rough. I waited there, holding the gun and not moving for half an hour. Eyes wide, I stayed ready. Nothing. I wanted to turn on a light, but I was too scared. My legs were cramping.

Finally, I convinced myself that it was a false alarm, clicked the safety back on again, put the gun away, and lay back down. I covered my head and tried to sleep, but I was still panicking.

Just go to sleep! This is ridiculous. No one is there. There's no face. I'm just hearing things. My heart is pounding. I'm sweating. I keep seeing him, the silhouette, barging in here, pushing me down on the bed. Who is he? I would shoot him. No one is here. Dear God, please help me sleep. God I'm so tired, please just help me fall asleep and not be scared. If someone was going to break into one of these condos, they wouldn't choose mine. I'm all the way on the top floor! I'm safe. Why do I feel so terrified?

I watched TV for a couple more hours and finally fell back asleep around dawn when the Benadryl took over. This had been a fairly typical night. Although the gun gave me a sense of security, it didn't stop the feelings. I couldn't stop the fear. In fact, it seemed to worsen.

Wednesday I was detailed to Brookside station. I loved going there. Good crew, nice apparatus, an upscale emergency response area. There was a Starbucks nearby and plenty of places for lunch. Best of all, I'd get to hang out with Cole, who was assigned to Engine 591.

It's not like she and I were best friends. We didn't call each other on the phone to chat, and didn't spend much time together outside of work. But I always looked forward to running into her, whether on a call, at some training, or when we were detailed to the same station. She was one of my favorite co-workers.

It was obvious that Cole is gay; she's a pretty tomboy. She has a great smile and loves to joke around. I'm always guaranteed to hear some good drama about one of the inter-county relationships going on, likely with a girl at another station. Or maybe someone she saw over the weekend. Either way, I knew there would be a story.

Around 5:45 a.m. I showed up, and Cole rolled in right behind me.

"Whatup girl!" I shouted.

"Hey Gina," she hollered back with a huge smile.

We hugged and acknowledged how fun it was going to be to run calls together that day.

We checked out the engine and EMS equipment, got the house duties done, and had already run a few calls by 10am. The medic crew was hanging out in the kitchen deciding what we should get for lunch, our engine guys were reading the paper, and Cole and I were sitting in the lounge catching up on the latest in County love life.

Somehow we got to talking about our families. I knew quite a bit about hers already, including that she had been raised in Maryland, in a sheltered environment with no TV.

"When I finished high school," she said, "I went to live with this couple who were friends of my parents that I had known since childhood."

"Uh huh?"

"And the man used to do things to me," she said. "I've been having such a hard time with it."

"What?"

I don't know what to say. I don't want to hear this. Please, stop. Stop it right now.

"He would make me do stuff… like, have sex with me and stuff."

Oh my gosh. I knew she was going to say that. Gross. Please don't go on.

"Wasn't he married?" I asked.

That was a stupid question! What am I saying?! The poor girl.

"Yes, he was. But it didn't matter. He treated me like I was his girlfriend."

"Holy sh*."

"I know."

"Didn't his wife do anything to stop it?"

"No."

"Did she know?"

"I don't know."

"No way!"

"Yeah. I think she just accepted it."

"That's crazy. I can't believe this."

"I've been seeing a counselor and stuff."

"That is so messed up, Cole!"

"I know, isn't it?"

Cole was not the verbose type. She just said it how it was. She went on to give me more details about what happened, and throughout the story her expression was as if she was telling me the address of a local building. No feeling whatsoever. Just facts. She was completely numb.

"I don't even know what to say," I said. "I'm sorry!"

I need to get out of here. This is a horrible story. This is too much. Why would she be telling me this? I feel so uncomfortable.

She kept talking. I wanted her to stop. I didn't want to hear it. Suddenly, I didn't like her as much. I didn't want to spend time with her anymore, but at the same time I felt sorry for her and cared for her deeply. It was as if I was so upset by what I was hearing that I couldn't deal with it. I just wanted it to stop.

"They traveled quite a bit," she continued. "And when he was away on a trip, he would write me letters. There was never anything weird in the letters or anything, and because he was a friend of the family, it all seemed normal. But, he took a special interest in me. At the time, I thought it was just neat to get the letters, you know?"

"Yeah, I can understand that," I said.

"I was finishing up high school," she continued, "and he talked me into coming to live with him and his wife in

Arizona. I thought it was my chance to go out and see the world. Little did I know that he was going to brainwash me, molest me, and not let me leave."

I switched gears internally. Don't listen. Don't feel it. Be practical. Nod and agree.

"His wife worked during the day," she continued, "and he was at home with me. He was a leader in the community, a person I trusted. He was traveling the world to 'help' people, and then he would come home and treat me like his whore."

"Oh my gosh." I wouldn't let myself feel it.

"I know. He was angry and controlling. I wasn't allowed to have friends. He would pick me up after school and control where I went and who I was with. He made me wear a ring, and I remember at the beach one time letting it wash off my finger."

"Did your parents find out?" I asked.

"My sister had a baby, and I wanted to come home for that. He didn't want me to leave, but I did anyway. While I was home, he called me all the time. Once, I didn't know my mom was listening on the phone, and he was talking some stuff. That's how my mom found out."

"Did she do anything about it?"

"Not really. She was mad at both of us."

"What about your dad?"

"He pretended like nothing was wrong at all."

"So what did you do?"

"I went back."

"Really? What made you go back?"

"He kept telling me I needed to make something of my life – something more than being a firefighter. He brainwashed me. It's not like he told me he loved me or anything. He just controlled me."

"You're here now. So, how did you get away?"

"We had a death in my family, and he wouldn't let me leave to come up for the funeral. But finally my dad sent me a plane ticket and told him that I had to come home. He couldn't refuse my dad, because they were friends."

"Did they stay friends?"

"Yes, that's the most messed up part! My parents stayed friends with them after what he did!"

"I don't get it."

"I know."

"I still feel guilty for not being around when my family needed me. I was terrified and guilty. Anyway, I stayed home after that. He kept trying to contact me, asking me to write him at a post office box or to call him during the day, of course when his wife was at work. Once I wrote him a letter and asked him why he did what he did. He never answered. I still have nightmares that he's there. I'm always angry in my dreams, and I want to just beat him. But I can never get to him."

"That is crazy."

"I know. And there's something else, too. When I was around six, my parents had this kid from New York come to our house for two weeks in the summer, and he tried stuff on me. I told my mom, and she took me to the doctor to make sure everything was okay down there, but that was it. My dad acted as if nothing ever happened."

"No way!"

"Yes. And they invited him back! They let him keep coming back! They kept in touch with him."

My jaw dropped. "Why the hell would they invite him back?!"

"I know. Can you believe it? And, you know, I'm not the way they want me to be. I've tried to be with a man, and I can't! I can't stand touching a man or being with him. I hate it. And they won't accept that I'm gay. We don't talk about it like as if it's some secret. I guess they felt if we kept quiet about it, it wouldn't be true."

"Being gay is against their religion right?" I asked, with a smirk.

"Exactly," she said, "But sexual abuse is perfectly fine, right?"

We both laughed nervously to diminish the depth of our discussion.

This is too much to take in.

"So I learned to keep secrets," she said. "Because no one wants to hear the truth."

There was no way I could stop. *Why did I drink so much! Everything is spinning. Open your eyes. That will help. Breathe. I'm so dizzy. Breathe. I have to puke. God, I'm so sorry. I'm so horrible. Stop spinning. Drink some water. I'm going to do better. I'm trying to be a good person. Why do I do this all the time? I hate myself.*

I went into the bathroom and puked. *Oh, that's better.* Puked again. I still felt so wasted, so I jammed my fingers down my throat and made myself puke until there was nothing more.

Back in bed, I was too sick to be scared. Sick and sick of feeling sick. I was back and forth between bed and the bathroom until 5:30am. I took at least three burning showers,

each time feeling a bit more sober and a lot more guilt, and I
threw up 10 or 15 times.

Good thing I'm off today.

*God, I'm so sorry about last night. I don't know what
I was thinking. I don't even remember what happened. Why
did I eat those leftovers when I got home! I feel so sick. I'm so
fat.*

As I had done hundreds of times before, I started to
re-hash a lifetime of embarrassments and mistakes and blame
myself for everything, including getting drunk last night. I
criticized my every imperfection until I was beaten down to
nothing.

*My parents have no idea who I really am and how I
feel. Underneath those straight A's, I'm a disaster. This stupid
heart tattoo that I got when I was seventeen. How can I make
it disappear? Stealing that Santa Claus. I wonder if those
people saw me return it. All of those parties. Getting drunk
practically every night since age 17. Smoking cigarettes.
Stealing street signs for fun.*

*I wish there was a way I could just be the real me, but
they would freak. I'm just dying to be myself. I would like to
just be accepted and not feel so much pressure to be perfect.
What does 'being myself' even mean? Do I talk about how
hard I think life is? Do I just swear in front of them? What's*

that going to accomplish? I feel like I'm keeping so much inside. What is it that I want to say? What should I do? It's not their fault that I'm not myself; it's mine. Why don't I just talk to them? I'm too scared they won't approve.

Look what I put them through when I got married at Jimmy Buffett's Margaritaville when I was nineteen! They were devastated. They didn't even know who he was. Either did I, for that matter. And then that whole ugly divorce process three months later. None of my new friends know about that whole thing. I don't want anyone to know. I wish I could just erase that entire part of my life. I hate so much of my life.

What kind of person am I? I'm not that bad! I thought I would be dead by now. I wish it wasn't a sin to kill yourself. Why do I act the way I do? I'm so ashamed of myself. Look at how fat my face is. I hope I don't look as fat tomorrow. What if I went to jail? Look at my skin. Why am I such a mess? Drink some water.

Everyone was probably talking about how I locked up the brakes on the tanker yesterday. That wasn't my fault! I should have known. Damn it, I must have looked like such an idiot trying to extinguish the smoking brakes. You don't put water on hot tires! They could have burst and killed someone.

I'm an idiot. Captain is going to freak out on me on Monday. Everyone is going to know.

How did I screw up on that ALS protocol practical last Wednesday? I know those things inside and out. Dumb ass. I rushed it. I forgot to check for pedal edema. They're going to be talking about that all week at the station.

I can't believe that ladder fell. It was up there. It looked straight. Man, that hurt when it bounced off the concrete. Look at that scar under my nose. Like I really need another scar.

I have to puke.

The whole night went by like this, as it did every time. I was guilty, I felt guilty, I felt horrible, I felt like such a bad person. I wanted to just forget it all and be normal. I filled the tub with scorching hot water, stumbled into it and laid down.

I wish I could drown. Right now. Just end it. ˎ

I rolled over onto my stomach and stuck my face into the water and held my breath. I stared into the whiteness.

I can't die like this, naked in the tub. First of all, what the hell is going to kill me, the bubbles? Secondly, the last thing I want is some EMS crew with people that I know seeing me nude. Third, I'll go to hell. Definitely don't want that! God, I'm so sorry. Please forgive me for being an idiot.

I slept most of the next day and ate a bagel to absorb the beer and shots. By evening, I had a more realistic attitude about work and figured that my mistakes were nothing in comparison to a lot of what happens in the County.

No one is going to really care. But I care. I gotta get my sh* together. Can't make mistakes like that. I'm so hard on myself. But if only I could stop screwing up, I wouldn't have to go through this. When am I going to learn? Why do other people have it so easy, and I have it so tough?

Night came, and I was tired. The guilt was back. And so was the fear. It was the same staggering dread all over again. My promise to myself was always the same: Change. Improve. Stop embarrassing yourself. Do something more so that people will look up to you. Achieve. Get moving. Start over. You can do better.

It was Friday, and I had scheduled lunch with the Battalion Chief to let him know what was going on.

"I put in my resignation letter this morning," I said.

"What?!"

"Yeah, I'm going to start doing the technology stuff full time."

"Really. Well the department is sure going to miss you."

"Ha ha, yeah right," I giggled nervously, unable to accept his flattery.

I can't even believe I ever came to work here. What was I thinking?

"Gina, we've been so lucky to have you. I know you really like working on your web development, and I think it's great that you've found something you enjoy, but we'll miss you."

"You know, my parents both worked in IT consulting, and I first worked for a systems integrator when I was seventeen, over the summers up in Jersey. In college, I jumped from computer science to English, to French, to music, and I landed in this fire service industry pretty much due to job market factors and weird luck. Anyway, now that I've been through it, I think that fire and rescue is really a man's job," I said.

"Why do you say that?"

"Well, I'm not saying women shouldn't do it. I did it," I smiled. "But, I work out every single day. I run for an hour, then I lift for an hour, I eat flawlessly, and I still can't physically do what even the weaker guys can do. My body breaks down the muscle. A guy's body builds it up. They're just made for it."

"You do a great job."

"Well, it's not good enough."

I can never accept compliments.

"I think this career is for young, strong, tall men," I continued. "Don't get me wrong. I love being an engine driver – that's a perfect assignment for me, but it's time to move up, and I can't see myself in an office position. What I love about this job is actually running calls and helping people. And the truth is, a guy could do it a lot better than I can."

"There are plenty of other aspects to the job that are vital that have nothing to do with physique," he said, with his hands open wide. "What about critical thinking? Incident management, assessment and mitigation. You have exceptional aptitude. In the Tech II promotional process, you ran the incident like a pro."

"Anyway," I smiled, "I think I'll do a lot better in IT."

"Well, I wish you the best of luck. Who are you going to be doing work for?"

"I have several things lined up, all web work, design and branding type stuff. I think I'll be doing some work at Firehouse.com in the news room, doing web design and advertising. I'll probably also work on an e-commerce implementation for that ticket broker in D.C."

"Are you and your brother still going to record music?"

"Probably now and then," I said.

"Well, send me your CDs if you do. And keep in touch. I know you'll do great."

"Thanks. I'm sure Doug will keep you in the loop on what I'm doing."

On December 13, 2000, Doug and I were slouched on the couch, staring in amazement at channel 7 as Al Gore conceded the election to George W. Bush. We had just returned from a dinner out with friends, I had already taken a bath and was in my red footie pajamas drinking decaf hot tea.

I was mesmerized by the whole chad thing – dimpled, pregnant, hanging – how our presidential election had become a farce. A commercial came on, and Doug muted the TV. He leaned over and said, "Gina, I love you and love spending time with you. You're my best friend, and I want us to be together for the rest of our lives. I would love it if you would marry me." Then he reached under the couch, pulled out a diamond ring and asked, "Will you be my wife?"

I held the ring and began to bawl.

It's beautiful. Platinum. Great choice.

I didn't move, I didn't look at him, I didn't answer. I just cried.

He doesn't really want to marry me. He's just doing this for me. He doesn't want to be with me. He's not sincere. What am I going to do? I love him. I really love him. What if he doesn't really love me? I'm so unsure of how he feels about me. We've been together for five years. I should know by now. What if he isn't sure? If he really loved me, he would have asked me sooner.

I couldn't answer. I wanted to answer.

Say yes! Say yes!

"Are you sure you want to be with me?" I asked.

"Of course I'm sure."

I just cried more. And more. I wept for over an hour. I couldn't respond appropriately, I couldn't talk about anything else, and I couldn't come up with the answer. Despite wanting to marry him more than anything, I couldn't believe that he would want to be with me.

What if later on he rejects me? What if I'm making a big mistake?

It wasn't until the next morning that he had an answer. I was talking to my friend Katherine on the phone, and I said, "Guess what? Doug and I are getting married!"

Doug overheard us and said sarcastically, "Oh, we are?"

"Yes, we are," I said. "I'm sorry, honey. I'm just so worried that you don't really love me and that you're doing this for me, not because you really want to. I'm also worried about your kids. Will you please check with them and make sure they're okay with this decision? Make sure they'll accept me as a step-mom?"

"Yes, I will," he assured me.

We talked through things and agreed that we were both ready.

V alley Lakes is a perfectly-planned neighborhood – beautiful homes, a community center and pool, walking trails, a pond and pristine landscaping along an inviting stone entrance. I was excited to see my friend Anne, her husband Greg and their new house. Anne and I had worked together at TGI Friday's in Tysons from age nineteen through twenty-one, and we made a living restaurant-hopping together for a few years following that. We've always lived within fifteen minutes of each other, yet our different lifestyles make it a challenge for us to connect and spend quality time on a regular basis.

Greg was unpacking the last of their boxes from the van when we pulled up.

"Hey," Anne smiled at me, and we hugged.

"So good to see you!" I said.

Doug and Greg shook hands, and Anne and I quickly took advantage of the opportunity to chat while the guys took over the lifting.

"Let me see the ring!" she said. "Congratulations! Aren't you so happy?"

"Yeah, I really am."

"Come inside," she said. "Let's get a soda, and I'll show you around."

The place was gorgeous, and I was immediately wondering how they could afford it.

She gave me a tour, and showed me all of the work she had done. Awesome painting and great decorating, as usual. I loved how you had to step up to the master bedroom and walk through double doors. It was so spacious, new and clean.

"What a great place for you guys and the kids to grow up, huh?" I asked.

"Yeah, they love it," she said, as we walked down the hall. "This is their playroom."

She proceeded to show me their furniture, toy chests, and the wall color that her oldest son had picked out.

"You're amazing," I said. "You've done so much decorating already. Moving is so much work, isn't it?'

"Yeah, it sucks! Thank God my parents are watching the boys right now. So how are you and Doug doing?"

"We're great. You know. Things are good."

"Do you think you guys are ever going to have kids?" she asked.

"Anne! We just got engaged!"

"I know, but, I mean, down the road."

"I'm already going to be a step-mom. I think that's going to be enough."

"Yeah, but don't you want to have a baby?"

"I don't know. I mean, I feel like sometimes I can barely handle my own life. Plus, I think a lot of people step into parenthood without really realizing how much of a responsibility it is. Keeping your kids safe, taking care of them, shaping who they are, you know? Some days I feel like it's all I can do to take care of myself."

"Oh my God, you would be the best mother ever, Gina."

"I don't know. I don't think I could do it. I have it made – two great step-kids, a boy and a girl. What more could I ask for?"

"You gotta have a baby. It's the best experience ever. I just don't understand if you're not going to have a kid, then what's your meaning in life?"

Wow. "I don't think I have to have a baby to have meaning, do I? There are other things."

"Really? Like what? Work?" she snickered, not intending to be mean, I'm sure, but pointing out my workaholic ways.

"Just my everyday interactions. I think I can make a positive impact on the people and children I come into contact with everyday, without the need to bring more of them into the world. You know, when I think back to elementary school, I found things really difficult. Maybe it's just me, but I wouldn't want to put another child through that. That's where I am right now."

"I guess I just don't understand why not. I think you would be so happy and so great as a mom."

"How about if I start by getting married, and then I can go from there," I said sarcastically, with a smile.

"Alright, alright, I'm giving up for now," she said, waving me downstairs in a motherly way. "I just finished decorating the basement. Let me show you."

"You've done such a great job here. The place is gorgeous!" I said.

Good God, it drives me crazy when she pushes me on the kid thing. She's been asking me that for two years, and I'm not even married yet. I don't want kids. Why would anyone

want to grow up in this scary world? Oh well, I know she
doesn't mean anything by it. She's a great friend. Let it go.

After the tour, we sat down on the steps to chat, reminiscing about old times waiting tables together, living at Rehoboth over the summers, and going dancing in DC.

"I don't know how we did it," I said.

"I know," she agreed, "we were so stupid."

"Yup. You know, I have so much anxiety over all of the stupid things I did in the past."

"You do?" she asked, scrunching her face up in shock.

"Yeah, I really do. I have this terrible guilt thing, and I feel nervous and anxious. It's starting to affect me at work."

"Really? Gina. I can't believe what I'm hearing! I've known you for like ten years, and I've always been the one who has the anxiety problems," she said.

"Well, I don't know what happened. I just feel really agitated, nervous and edgy a lot."

"Like, do you get panic attacks?" she asked.

"I don't know. Maybe."

"But you're always so confident and successful."

"I may look like it, but I don't feel like it."

"Maybe you should go to the doctor."

"Yeah, I've been thinking about it."

Doug and I left Anne and Greg's by 4 p.m., and we headed out to Flint Hill to see my soon-to-be in-laws.

Man this is a beautiful drive. Look at the hills, the trees, the fields. Turn up the music. Where's my Don Henley? What about Sarah McLachlan?

I switched the CD, cranked it and stared out the window, singing along.

I love this song. I wish Doug could know what it feels like, to get lost in music like this. He doesn't feel things the way I do.

I became the song and floated with the winds, across the hills, up the winding roads. I pushed my way through the wild yellow grasses blowing in the breeze.

I feel alone. Sing it. Turn it up.

I thought about the world and all of its complexities, the way people interact and don't understand each other. I thought about everything except where I was right then. I got as far lost as I could.

lanning the details of our wedding consumed me for the next year. It was Friday, October 5, 2001, and we were just four weeks away. Doug was still at work and wouldn't be home for hours. I was watching TV.

Why did that movie bother me so much? That Lifetime crap... it's garbage. That guy took his step-daughter out on his boat and made her touch him – how disgusting. That is so disturbing.

I went to take a bath, a really hot bath. I sat there thinking about the movie I just watched and my upcoming wedding.

It's only a month away!

That jerk better not come to the wedding. I don't want him around my step-kids or any of the kids, for that matter. Oh my gosh, what if he comes? That will ruin my day. This is supposed to be my day. He'll make me feel so nervous like he always does. What if he says something suggestive like he did at Mike's wedding? What if I start crying?

I feel terrified right now. What if someone breaks in? I need to call Doug. Let me turn the water hotter.

I started crying and shaking. I dunked down into the water so that my face was sticking up just enough to breathe. My skin was all red. My hair was hot.

I sat up and gripped the sides of the tub with my red pruney hands. The tiles were so cold. I felt panicked. I was sweating and crying more. I was having trouble breathing.

What if he turns up? Okay, quit thinking about the possibilities and take control. What if I call him and I threaten him? I'll just tell him that I don't want him there and that he better not show up. What will I say? What if he responds as if nothing ever happened. Oh my gosh, what if Doug finds out? He'll think I'm disgusting. Our relationship will be over. He won't want to marry me!

I was bawling. I panicked, going around and around in circles in my mind. I was trying to blow my nose and was crying more at the same time.

How am I going to keep him from showing up at my wedding? What did he do to me?! Why am I thinking about this? Stop. Oh my gosh. How old was I? Two? Three? Oh my gosh. Why did he do that? What the hell is going on!

The time I came out of the bathroom. The times I slept over there. When he was standing naked in Mike's room. I was so terrified. On the couch. In the kitchen. Oh my gosh, in our dining room at dinner. "Ma petite blonde" (my little girlfriend), he would say. Eww.

I shivered. I stared.

Why didn't anyone notice?

I got back in the tub and turned it on. Scorching water.

Clean me. Burn it away.

I couldn't catch my breath. My heart was pounding through my ears.

Focus. You have to figure out how to get him to decline the invitation. If I hadn't invited him and Aunt Marianne, that would have raised a red flag to my family. Now I have to make sure he doesn't accept. I put my hands together and sobbed.

God, please, please, please make sure Uncle Louis doesn't come to the wedding. Please, Lord. I know I'm not perfect, and I know I've done a million awful things in my life, but, God please.

I toweled off and got my act together. It was two
hours before Doug got home, and by the time he did, I looked
okay.

Just forget about it. Don't mention it.

Over the next week, the RSVPs kept coming in. Four
and five each day. But nothing from my aunt and uncle yet.

It was Sunday evening, and I couldn't wait any longer
to find out whether he was coming, so I called my mom.

"Hi mom?"

"Hi Gina," she sparkled back, as always – cheerful
and loving.

"Have you heard anything from your sisters on who is
coming to the wedding?"

"I think Auntie Gabrielle and Uncle Derek are the
only ones coming from my side. You know no one in Quebec
really has the money to spend on a trip like that."

"That's fine, I know."

What about them? They have enough money.

"What about Tante Marianne and Oncle Louis?" I
asked, begging for a "no."

"Tante Marianne really wants to come, but Oncle
Louis refuses to fly. So she would have to take several days
off work in order to drive down, and she's not sure if she's
going to be able to."

"I don't want Uncle Louis to come anyway," I blurted. I was sweating, lying down on my bed, staring at the ceiling and gripping the phone. I was trying to escape.

"You don't? Why not?"

I shouldn't have said anything.

"I don't like him."

"Really? That's the first time I've ever heard that."

"He's just a jerk. Remember that whole thing about him trying to kiss Viviane?"

"Yes."

"I think that's horrible. I don't want him around the kids."

"Okay, well I'm pretty sure he won't be coming. Tante Marianne said that he absolutely refuses to fly. Can you believe that?"

Phew.

"Why is that? Is he afraid of a plane crash or something?" I asked.

"I don't know. He's just scared of flying."

"Okay. Alright, well I'll talk to you later."

"I love you, Gina."

"Love you too, Mom."

Work could not have been busier than it was on this Monday morning. I was at the Firehouse.com office in College Park, working on their web site.

Okay, I'm going to have to just call them and make sure they're not coming. If they are, then I'll have to stop them. Why in the world is she with that disgusting loser anyway? He's awful. I'm not waiting any longer for their RSVP.

I grabbed my cell and dialed Montreal. In college, I used to call her office number frequently, and we would chat.

I never once even thought about it back then. Deep denial, I guess. Why is it coming back like this? I can't stop thinking about it. Why can't I just forget about him? What an ass!

"Oui bonjour?"

"Hi Tante Marianne, it's Gina."

"Oh hi," she replied, lightly pronouncing the 'H' like the French do. "It's been a while, eh? How are you, little Gina?"

Okay, I'm 30 now, not exactly little anymore, but whatever.

"I'm pretty good." I had the editor leaning over my cube and lifting his glasses like he had a hot new story that needed to go up on the web immediately. I acknowledged him and motioned that I would swing by in a minute.

"How is the wedding planning going?"

"It's good." I suddenly didn't like her. All these years, I loved her, and now I felt angry. But I sounded as sweet as ever.

"I don't think Oncle Louis and I are going to be able to come, Gina."

"Oh that's okay. I know it's far and everything." *Sweet.* I didn't feel all that relieved yet, maybe because I had to pretend I was disappointed.

"We would like to send you something special that you can remember us by. Can you think of anything?"

"You don't need to get us anything, really. That's so nice of you."

I don't want to remember him.

"But we want to, we really do."

"Well, we are registered, you know. There are tons of things that we need for the house."

"But Gina we want to get you something unique from us. Oncle Louis and I love you so much."

Eww. I hate his guts, and I don't want a gift from him. He makes me sick.

"Well, let me think about it. I'll let you know, okay?"

"Okay." She paused long enough for me to feel a sigh of relief.

It's actually happening. He's not coming!

"So, how's your weight doing?" she asked.

It took less than 2 seconds for my eyes to well up. I was pissed.

How could she ask me that!

"No more weight gain problems?"

"No, it's going good," I replied, barely getting the words out. Tears were pushing their way out of my eyes. I was nervous, embarrassed and angry. I flashed back to high school when I would go up to Quebec to visit the family. "You've gained weight" or "you've lost weight," they would remark in French as soon as they saw me, then give me a big hug and giggle. I'd smile and blow it off. But it hurt. It really hurt.

What the hell is so important about my weight?! You know why I keep gaining weight?! Because of your stupid f*ing husband. B*tch. There are a lot of things that are more important than the way a person looks! Why don't you ask how I'm doing inside? Don't you care about how I'm feeling? I hate the way I look. Why do you have to remind me?

"That's great that you've been able to keep your weight down. Is your dress all ready, and it fits well?"

F* this discussion.

"Yeah, the dress is awesome," I answered quietly, again barely able to get the words out. I covered the phone, cleared my throat, and got my sh* together. "Listen, I just wanted to say hi quickly, but I'm at work, and I gotta go. I love you!" I said sweetly, the tears still flowing.

"Okay Gina, I love you too. By-bye."

I rolled my chair back and charged out of the office, ran down the stairs to another floor and barged into the bathroom. I leaned on the sink. *Dammit it's wet.*

Oh my God. She has no idea how that makes me feel. Why does she do that? Okay, thank God they're not coming. Everything's going to be fine. Thank you, God.

I took a wet paper towel to my eyes. I looked in the mirror.

People are so mean.

For a few more years, I continued consulting and working for small firms until I reached the point where, in order to grow, I would need to either take a financial risk and invest in my business or go work for a larger and more stable company and figure out how professional businesses operate.

I chose the "real job" route and, over the next 5 years, jumped around from web site design to internet media, web advertising, teaching IT courses at a career college, and eventually landed in IT professional services. I dove into every position in full learning mode, absorbing as much as I could. I worked long hours, almost every weekend, and always two or more jobs at a time.

I began an intense journey toward success.

This is only temporary. I just need to be successful, and then I can slow down. I'm doing a good thing here, preparing for my future.

First, I needed to learn the technical stuff. Then, I needed to learn the business. As soon as I reached one step, it was time to advance to the next. At first, I just needed to make ten thousand more, then twenty, then twice as much. And the responsibility and money was never enough because I could do more.

Soon, I'll get where I need to be, and then I can slow down and enjoy life. I need to keep going at this pace until I reach success. Maybe I can retire early.

One Christmas Day, I decided that I needed to get a better grip on the latest business trends and that a Master's Degree would be next on my list. I signed up for the GMAT online and took it at 8am the next day. In March, I started my Master of Science in the Management of IT program at UVΛ's McIntire School of Commerce. During the next 16 months I worked full time, did some side consulting, read and studied every night, went to class on Saturdays, and worked on school projects on Sundays.

At work and at school, no matter what I did, it was never good enough in my own mind. In every meeting, interview, or working session, I felt like a kid – unaware of

what everyone else knew, and lacking confidence. I had
become extremely uncomfortable being in any group settings
– whether in class, in meetings, or socially. I always felt self-
conscious and was sure that everyone was criticizing me all
the time. I had a well developed characteristic of being
outspoken and cracking jokes in an effort to distract people
from seeing the real me. And, I'm quite sure that few had a
clue that I was anything but confident.

Nights before class, I couldn't sleep. I was so
concerned that I didn't know the course materials inside and
out. I was worried that I'd oversleep or that I wouldn't have
answers to the professor's questions. I hated the way I looked
and ran countless negative scenarios, potential critical
comments, and judgments over and over in my mind
throughout the day. My eyes were always bloodshot.

On class days – just like business meeting days – I
would usually arrive late because I had spent too much time
obsessing over my looks – my skin, my hair, my clothes. I had
to look nice, but it couldn't draw attention or comments. It
couldn't be anything too new or too noticeable. I didn't like to
be looked at and, yet, I wanted to look perfect but knew I
never would.

I was unable to participate in class much, because, in
my mind, I had nothing valuable to say. Everyone there was

better than me, smarter than me, and more confident. I tried to participate at times but usually experienced such nervousness and discomfort that it just wasn't worth it. I felt my face turn burning red, I would sweat, and my voice would shake. I was typically able to hide the nervousness in a distracting joke, but, still, I was a wreck inside.

Despite the internal agony, I loved the education. My masters degree enabled me to work more effectively with clients, with my team, and when making business decisions. Between the day I started and graduation day, I had landed a new job with an exciting company and was promoted into what I considered an ideal role – working with clients to evaluate their challenges and frame IT solution development or business strategy engagements. I dropped all part-time consulting work and focused on finishing up my graduate degree and successfully kicking off this new career.

Two hours had passed since we turned off the TV. I was thinking about work.

"Honey, stop kicking your legs around," Doug said.

"I can't help it. I can't relax."

"Don't you think you should go to the doctor? You have all this trouble sleeping, you're restless, you worry so much, and you don't feel good. I'm sure you could get something to help."

"I know. I'll make an appointment."

It had to be the tenth time that I made that promise and never followed through. I didn't want to go to the doctor. I didn't want to have to lie.

I barely slept that night and was so irritated in the morning that I decided the doctor would happen now or never, so I called to get an appointment.

"What did you want to see the doctor for today?" the receptionist asked.

"I can't sleep," I said.

"Okay, have you had insomnia before?"

"Yes, for quite a few years. It's just to the point now that it's really interfering with my life."

Not to mention drinking cough syrup or taking Benadryl to fall asleep ever since age nineteen.

"We have a 10:15 opening."

"Perfect, I'll see you then."

I missed the turn on the way and pulled into the parking lot at 10:17. I was cursing myself the whole way there for not leaving the house earlier.

I'm sweating and late. They're going to think I'm unorganized. They won't let me have my appointment. I look messy. They'll probably think I'm lazy and don't work. Do I stink?

I signed in at the desk, and they didn't say anything about me being late. A few minutes later, the physician's assistant called me in.

She weighed me, measured me, and did the standard interview.

"So you're having trouble sleeping?" she asked.

"Yeah. I can't relax. I've been taking Tylenol PM pretty frequently, but I still have a lot of trouble. Then, I'm exhausted in the morning, and I have a hard time getting up. I'm tired during work, and I feel like I'm going to fall asleep a lot."

"Okay, let me get your vitals, and the doctor will come in and see you in a few minutes."

I lay down on the noisy paper-covered exam chair under hideous fluorescent lighting and read through People magazine. Knowing that I was about to get help, I felt better and almost fell asleep.

Dr. Tarrington knocked twice, and I quickly sat up and pretended to be alert. She entered, looking fresh and smart as usual.

"Hello there, how are you doing?" she said, as if she remembered everything about my medical history.

She probably thinks I'm crazy and make up illnesses.

"I'm pretty good. How are you?" I smiled, as always.

"Oh, good," she said. "Having trouble sleeping, are you?"

"Yes. My husband complains about my restlessness, the fact that I kick my legs around at night, how I can't relax, can't fall asleep, and wake up all the time."

"What is it that keeps you awake?"

"My brain. I always worry about stuff."

"So you're anxious?"

"Yeah, I think so. Nervous and worried."

"What are you anxious about?"

"Mostly work. I have a lot of pressure, and I get really tense when I have big meetings or deliverables. I guess I'm pretty much anxious all the time. I'm stressed out because I've been working on a lot of things at the same time. I'm also in grad school, and it's kicking my butt."

"What do you do?"

"I work for a technology consulting firm. Recently I've had a lot of changes at work, and the pressure right now is overwhelming. I think I'm just trying to do too much at the same time."

"When you get anxious, what do you think about?"

"I'm hard on myself. I worry what other people think of me and obsess about doing a good job. I just want things to go well. I feel like right now it's too much to handle."

"Are you depressed?"

"I don't think so."

"What have you been doing to help yourself with the anxiety?"

"I take a lot of baths," I smiled, "and I sit on the couch and drink tea. I also take Tylenol PM at night to help me sleep.

Other than that, all I can do is constantly try to tell myself that things will be okay. When I get really anxious, I just talk myself into calming down."

"Do you feel suicidal at all?"

"No, I'm not suicidal."

I'm not suicidal at all. Why would she ask me that?!

"Although, a lot of times, I wish I wasn't alive, because the stress is just too much to deal with. But, because of my faith, I believe it would be wrong for me to kill myself, so I would never do it." I smiled to show her I was normal.

"So, you do fantasize about dying though?"

"Well, I don't know about fantasizing. I do think about ways to escape the anxiety. It just feels like life is too much for me to bear sometimes. It's more like I wish that someone would crash into me or drive me off the road and cause me to die, or something."

"Let's see, you're thirty-three now, hmm?"

"Yes."

"And how long has this been going on?"

"I've sort of always been anxious. But this is the first time that the level of anxiety has become unbearable and has begun to interfere with my work. It really kicked off in the spring when I started grad school, so it's been about eight months, I guess."

"Well, the first thing I would recommend is that you would get some counseling, and I'll give you the name of someone local who you could try. Secondly, if you're experiencing this level of anxiety, maybe you would like to try something like Prozac or Zoloft, which are mostly for depression but have shown to be effective for anxiety."

We went through the different options, and I chose Zoloft based on a friend of mine having taken it for post-partum depression and anxiety with good results.

"Can't I take something like Xanax for the anxiety? I've only tried it once, but it really worked."

"The problem with Xanax, Gina, is that it's highly addictive. You don't want to get to the point where you rely on it."

"Okay."

I definitely don't want to get addicted. I can see that happening way too easily.

I stopped at the pharmacy on the way home and couldn't wait to try this Zoloft stuff. I would have been willing to try anything.

I don't want to tell Doug that it's an anti-depressant, because then he'll think I'm crazy. I don't want our relationship to fall apart.

As I turned into Saybrooke and neared our house, I popped my first Zoloft. Within just a few minutes, my chest felt tight and my heart was beating fast. I felt nervous and uncomfortable.

You're just over analyzing this. It's probably your imagination. Go take a bath. Relax.

I immediately went inside and up to bed. I fell asleep before Doug came home.

Around midnight, I woke up, my heart pounding. I suddenly became filled with rage. I mean, I was so angry that I was afraid of what I would do. I looked over at Doug, who was sleeping, and I had this urge to smash his face in. And it wasn't just an urge, it was a violent vision. I could see it happening, and I wanted it to stop, but I couldn't make it.

What the hell is going on?! I love him. Stop thinking these horrible things! Why is this happening? I should wake him up and tell him. No! He'll think I'm crazy. Oh God, what do I do? I feel like I'm going to kill him. Take that fist and bash it into his face. Smash his nose right through his head. Smash it again. Look at the blood all over your hands. It's all over the place. This is terrifying. Don't move. Relax. Do not move. You're not going to hurt anyone. It's the medication. Am I asleep or awake? I pinched myself, like I've seen in the movies. Yup, definitely awake. I'm furious. Breathe.

I stayed still for two hours. Finally, I fell asleep but had scary, violent dreams that seemed real. By mid-morning, I seemed to feel more normal. I called Doug and explained that I didn't sleep well with the medication, that I had had bad dreams, and that there was no way I was going to take it again.

"Oh well, you tried," he said, encouragingly. "Maybe there's something else."

"Yeah, maybe."

I think I'll stick to being stressed for now. No medication. That was scary!

Walking into work that day was beyond awkward. The medication was wearing off, but I still didn't feel like myself. My colleague Rob and I went for coffee, and I opened up to him a little bit about how enraged I felt toward Doug after taking that medication.

"I think I realized how much hidden anger I have, you know?" I said. All he could muster up was a "wow," and I didn't blame him.

I shouldn't be talking about this right now. Keep it to yourself.

I didn't go back to the doctor for over a year. I also never called the counselor because I had no idea what it would be like and was sure that it wouldn't help with my anxiety.

This stuff must be for psychotic people. I'm normal. I'm just stressed. I can handle it. I can handle anything. Some counselor who works with crazy people isn't going to be helpful to me. And this medication is obviously not appropriate for my state of mind. It practically turned me into a maniac.

Leah, my little next door neighbor, was playing outside when I pulled into the driveway from work. She stood and waited like a statue while I parked my car and then ran over at full toddler speed to give me a hug. "Miss Gina, Miss Gina," she said, throwing her arms around me. "Would you like to play with me?"

I loved Leah. Her curly blonde hair, her tiny little adorable self – all smiles, silly faces and giggles. Leah was so full of life, and she made me feel alive. She liked to act just a little bit crazy, cracking herself up, and she reminded me of the girl I used to be before I grew into all of this anxiety. I liked to treat Leah the way I wanted to be treated at that age.

So, we hung out. She would come over and have dinner with Doug and me sometimes, and other times we played outside, checking out the bugs, walking through our garden and pointing out the prettiest flowers, and doing sidewalk chalk. We talked, listened to music, and laughed like crazy. Leah made me feel calm, and she made me appreciate myself without judgment.

Now three years with the same company, I was
satisfied with where I was in my career. For the
first time since age nineteen, I was only working one job, and
I wasn't looking for anything else. I knew that I would
eventually grow more and move up, but for now I was
enjoying my work and wanted to stay put. The money was
good, the work was good, the clients were good, and I began
to sense greater confidence in my professional ability as well
as my role within the company.

Successful business deals brought me a temporary
sense of satisfaction and happiness. And, the long hours and
hard work it took to win them helped me to escape from
facing the self that I didn't like. I had freedom and flexibility
in managing my own accounts and my portion of the business.
I was exceptionally motivated, genuinely liked working with

clients to help them be successful, and enjoyed eye-opening business conversations with C-level executives who had accomplished what I knew I would want to achieve next.

The flexibility of my schedule was key. Sometimes I was just too worn out to go in early. And by early, I mean 8:30 or 9:00 a.m. Because nights were usually rough for me, once I fell asleep, I needed to sleep in.

I also needed time off for doctor and dentist appointments. In one year, I had three cracked crowns. I thought the dentist was doing shoddy work. But, when I went to a new dentist to replace the third crown, she asked the right questions and discovered that I was grinding and biting so badly at night that I was cracking my own teeth. "On this one here, you've broken the tooth; it's not a crown. You need a night guard, and you need to wear it every night before you destroy these beautiful teeth," she said.

Thankfully, my colleagues and the company leadership were exceptionally bright, with great personalities and a sense of caring. Although I still felt different than them, it was as close to fitting in as I had ever experienced in a professional environment. I could joke about my stress level and anxiety, and people laughed along with me.

"My God, Gina. At this rate, you're going to have a heart attack by the time you're forty," one of my colleagues would say.

In 2005, Doug and I had bought a new home in Vint Hill, between Bristow and Warrenton, and we typically had evenings and weekends free to do whatever we wanted. We could afford to have housecleaning, laundry, grocery shopping and maintenance done for us, so, unless we really wanted to work on a project, we didn't have anything too burdensome on our plates.

Outside of work, I played music, decorated, gardened, and entertained friends. Doug's spare time was centered on riding and working on motorcycles. Over the months, as my comfort and interest in work increased, so did my dissatisfaction with our marriage.

I often sat home on weekends, feeling depressed. Doug was out having the time of his life riding dirt bikes with his friends, and I was stuck at home taking the few hours of relaxation that were available to me before I had to go back to another week of business headaches. I didn't have energy to do anything but recover from the previous week, and I resented his ability to take life easy and just have fun.

I started working out a lot again, and that improved my self-image. Soon, I was shopping more, getting massages, and doing things I enjoyed to take care of myself. But the burning emptiness inside wouldn't go away.

I felt alone. I felt that I had worked so hard all these years to become successful and that now I was alone in trying to enjoy it. Not only that, but I still had to work hard to maintain the lifestyle that we had, and although I knew Doug put his life on the line every day as a firefighter, I struggled far more than he did. I felt an uncomfortable and growing resentment toward him because he was happy, and I was not.

I had always been the sensitive one in our relationship, somewhat moody and extremely emotional about most discussions and decisions. Now, instead of having emotional talks, I shut down. I shut down for months and began to almost live a separate life.

On Sundays, he would go to a motorcycle race, and it didn't even seem to faze him that we would be apart all day. I would work late, and he didn't mind. What I wanted was for him to need me more, to miss me more, to want to be with me, and to want to talk. And from my perspective, he loved me in his own way but didn't really care all that much if we didn't spend a lot of quality time together. So, in my mind, he didn't really love me the way I needed him to.

Maybe he wants to be with me for the lifestyle. Maybe he likes the freedom. Although he loves me and cares about me, I'm sure he can't like me all that much. I'm a mess. We're so different. He doesn't understand me. No one understands me.

We'd been together for about eight years by then. And, nothing had changed except that, for me, life had slowed down. For the first time in my adult life, I had time on my hands – a lot of time. Maybe too much time to think. Slowing down made me evaluate who I really am and what I wanted.

I just want to get out of here. He'll be happier without me. He doesn't even want to be with me. We have practically nothing in common. I can't stand him anymore. He doesn't talk to me. He doesn't open up to me. He has nothing to say. He keeps everything inside. He doesn't express his feelings. I'm not sure if he even has any feelings.

I want him out of the house. I want to be here by myself and just stare out the window. I want him, his lack of depth, and his motorcycles out of my life.

What did I do? Why did I marry him? What am I doing? Why doesn't he love me?!

The blue chair on the left looked comfortable. I wondered how many people sat there and what they talked to her about.

This fabric is actually pretty gross. Kinda dirty. Oh good, she shut the door. I would hate to run into someone I know here.

Dr. Young started the conversation the same way as she would most sessions, "So, tell me. What's going on?"

"Well, I've been having problems with my marriage, and I think that some of the issues are my fault, and I thought it would be a good time to get some professional help from a psychotherapist."

"Okay, go ahead."

"I feel like my husband doesn't love me. We've been together for over 8 years now, married for 5, and we're struggling. I'm very passionate, very deep and emotional, extremely driven, and I enjoy intellectual conversations. My husband isn't anything like me. We don't communicate the way I want to, and he doesn't understand. He's happy talking about the weather, while I want to connect on a deeper level. I feel like my marriage is very empty."

"When I tell him I want to have a stronger connection with him, he says that he doesn't even understand what I mean. I try to explain that I want to talk about deep stuff – what is important to him, what he believes in, what he has experienced in life. He doesn't understand what he needs to talk about. He says he wants to be a better communicator, but he doesn't know what I really need. I feel like I never should have married him. We started out on a rocky path, and I'm regretting that I stayed on it."

Dr. Young and I talked about these issues for several sessions. We re-hashed everything Doug and I had been through – the good and the bad – and explored how things had changed over the years. We talked through our family histories and differences in how we were brought up. We kept coming back to the same issue – my desire for better communication and need for a greater emotional connection with him. I admitted that I was so fed up with the distance between us that I was on the verge of asking for a divorce.

"I feel like an idiot coming to you for this" I said.

She probably thinks I'm a whiny loser.

"What do you mean?" she asked.

"Well, I'm sure you have patients with real problems, and I'm complaining to you because my husband doesn't communicate the way I want him to. I'm typically a very good decision maker, and I can make logical choices. For the first time in my life, my decision to leave or to stay is really muddy. I'm extremely confused and can't make the decision. I feel like I'm wasting your time with this, but it's a real problem for me. I want to decide if I should stay married or go, and I can't even focus. I'm confused beyond my ability to evaluate the decision."

"That's fine," she said. "Your problems are worth talking about."

Wow. I wonder if she is just saying that.

"What else have you been thinking about?" she asked.

I have no idea what words I used. I don't remember what it was that made me trust her and trust myself enough to admit something that I had never before admitted to anyone aloud, including myself.

I just need to get it out. How the hell do I put this?

I explained it. Briefly. And I waited.

She waited to make sure I had said everything I wanted to say.

"I'm so sorry," she responded.

"It's okay," I smiled, as if I just told her about a splinter in my toe.

"You know," she said, "the level of anxiety that you've been experiencing, and the emotional issues you've been having with your husband – those are very common in cases of people who have suffered from childhood sexual abuse."

"They are?"

Holy sh*. What did she just say?

"Yes. With what you just told me about your uncle, you've developed some typical coping mechanisms for a victim of abuse."

I was suddenly unusually uncomfortable.

Sexual abuse? Was I really sexually abused? Is that what you call what that jerk used to do to me? I guess I always think of sexual abuse as someone who is tied up in a dungeon, tortured and beaten for twenty years. Am I a sexual abuse victim? No. I'm a successful business woman who has it all together. I'm a normal person. I want to go on with my life and be perfect. I can't possibly deal with this.

"So tell me how you're feeling."

"Gross," I said.

"What else?" she asked.

"Disgusting and dirty and nasty."

"What is disgusting and dirty and nasty?" she asked.

"I am."

"You're disgusting?" she asked.

"Yes. Well, it's what happened... the things he said and did to me."

"Do you feel ashamed of it?"

"Yes, totally. I feel embarrassed."

"How old were you when it first happened?"

"Young. Around two or three."

"And do you blame yourself?"

"Okay, I know it wasn't my fault at all, but I feel extremely humiliated about it, as if I was wrong. It makes me sick. I hate it, and I want it to go away. I know I didn't cause it, and for some reason even though I was so young, I felt that it was wrong and was very aware that I didn't like it, so I always tried to escape. I kicked and pushed and ran away when I could. But I still feel embarrassed and ashamed. I loved him, you know? Just like I loved all of my aunts and uncles. And the abuse was just a small part of our relationship, so it was so confusing! It's horrible. I'm so embarrassed about it that I can't even admit it. I've never told anyone this before."

"And how do you feel about it right now when you talk about it?" she asked.

"I don't know," I said. "I don't feel anything, really."

We spent the next half hour talking about the abuse, sort of without going too much into detail. I wasn't ready for that. She showed me a book and suggested that we could work through it together. It was a workbook for women survivors of sexual abuse.

Where can I hide this so that no one sees it?

I started seeing Dr. Young twice a week, during lunch and after work. I was a little surprised at the focus on sexual abuse. Now that I had talked about it, what more was there to do with it? My interest was in figuring out my marriage and whether I should stay or go. I couldn't stay in this cold, unfeeling relationship, yet I didn't trust my reasons for wanting to leave. I needed her to help me make a decision.

"What I really want to get out of this is help making a decision about my marriage. I've done the pros and cons analysis, and I just can't come to an answer. I'm so unable to feel propelled to move either way. This being in limbo is killing me, and I know it's not fair to my husband either," I said. "He deserves better."

"Okay, well we'll work on that."

Okay, good, 'cause that's all I care about right now.

Following was Dr. Young's initial treatment plan, as outlined in my official medical records:

Patient Name: Gina McCabe

Precipitant / "Why Now":

Not sure she wants to stay in marriage. Feels her life is not all it can be. Feels if she resolves own issues she will be able to better assess her marriage.

Presenting Problems (Current Symptoms, Evidence of Personal Distress, Impairment of Functioning):

Anxiety, tension, fatigue, depression, suicidal thoughts, excessive guilt, flash backs, memory problems, mood swings, anger, overall questioning meaning of her life, low self esteem repeated, OCD, sad.

Target Symptoms:

1)   Anxiety, panic, sleep – severe

2) Depression, suicidal thoughts – severe (for example "last night when I was really exhausted, I just wished I would go to sleep and never wake up. I feel like that all the time. I will never act on it though.")

3) Anger, tension – severe

4) Flash backs – severe

Mental Status:

Appearance - appropriate

Affect – Inappropriate laughter at times, out of anxiety as defense. Sad, angry, anxious.

Orientation – oriented

Mood – Depressed, angry

Thought Content – appropriate

Thought Process – logical

Speech – normal

Motor – normal

Intellect – above average

Insight – Partially present

Judgment – Normal

Impulse Control – normal

Memory – periods when anxious some difficulties

Concentration - periods when anxious some difficulties

Attention - periods when anxious some difficulties

Behavior – appropriate. Anxious, guarded

Thought Disorder – no problem

Relevant, Significant History of Presenting Problem:

Patient is a 35-year old professional woman with a Masters Degree in Management of Information Technology from University of Virginia. Now Director in technology consulting firm. Feels accomplished at her work, bright successful. Married to a firefighter (was herself a firefighter when she met husband).

Patient reported having a strong family base. Intact family, "loving wonderful family." Gets along with both parents. Strong bond with father, also previously a technical consultant, now retired. Mom was stay at home, taught French in the house, volunteered outside. One brother, 3 years older, married with one son.

Patient indicated husband is a good person, good at fixing things etc yet on a different level than her emotionally and intellectually. Patient reported that she was 31 when 9-11 happened, and she felt extremely anxious, upset for all the families of the victims.

Patient indicated that at age 19 she eloped, got married, and some weeks later "woke up" and got divorced. This decision was a source of guilt.

She met her current husband when she was 26 at work. Lying, cheating and deceit was traumatic for her in the beginning of their relationship. Before her wedding to him felt a lot of pressure, panic attacks, and then right before the wedding memories of sexual abuse by her uncle came up for her (she was between ages 2-7 when abuse occurred). She was terrified of the thought of him coming to the wedding and what it would be like if he came. That was the first time she acknowledged to herself that she was abused, broke through the denial. Remembering sitting in the bath tub crying about having to see him, felt very angry, felt like shooting him.

Also some sexual abuse by grandfather between ages 2-5.

Patient indicated she always seems to others as stable, outgoing, an achiever, good in school, yet inside experienced a sense of inferiority, never "good enough." As a child ages 5-9, remembers feeling sad a lot, sensitive with deep feelings, somewhat moody.

Patient reported that she drank heavily between ages 17-25 "wanting to escape." Now drinks "occasionally."

Relevant Information:

Father – anxiety, medications

Brother – PTSD (patient "does not know the story")

Treatment Plan / Measurable and Observable Goals / Solutions (How client will know therapy was successful):

1) Patient will start to work through sexual abuse and start to reclaim own power, feel less helpless, more hopeful, more in trust and control over own choices, less depressed.

2) Improve self understanding, self esteem, self forgiveness and develop plan of action.

Patient's Strengths & Resources:

A lot of own energy. Patient is an attractive woman, strong verbal communication, creative, warm, affectionate, caring.

Interventions:

Individual therapy to include bibliotherapy, CBT, sexual abuse, trauma work.

- Anger Management
- Imagery / Relaxation Training
- Stress Management
- Self / Other Boundaries Training
- Decision Option Exploration
- Pattern Identification and Interruption
- Facilitate Decision Making Regarding: marriage, sexual abuse
- Explore / Monitor: memories of abuse, impact, disclosure, actions

- Teach Skills of: communication regarding abuse, self comfort, acceptance, revealing of self
- Educate Regarding: sexual abuse patterns and coping
- Assign readings: The Courage to Heal
- Assign tasks of: working through feelings of "victim" toward empowerment

Treatment Plan Obstacles:

Need to control situation may affect ability to accept course of treatment.

Oh good. We're going to work on Decision Option exploration. Maybe I'll go home and make another pros and cons list. I need to set a deadline on this decision-making process. Poor Doug. He's a good guy, and he deserves better. He'll probably be so much happier without me.

The kids too. What kind of a step-mom am I, anyway, working all the time – on weekends, nights? I'm always at the computer. Always working on my career. I don't spend enough time with them.

This whole marriage thing was becoming really difficult. I had always thought that I was such a perfect wife. I was committed, loving, caring, affectionate, and a true friend. And yet, here I was going to therapy because I was on the verge of leaving.

I had told Doug that I didn't feel anything for him anymore. I didn't love him, and I didn't even like him. I was angry with him, and I felt that we never should have gotten together in the first place. I was bitter about the past, and I couldn't connect with him today. I needed more than he could give me, I was sure.

I went weeks without feeling anything. Completely numb. I wasn't happy, I wasn't sad, I wasn't anything. I wanted my body to float away into nothingness, because that's where I felt my soul was, anyway.

I wish I would just die. Why can't I just die of something.

Dr. Young had asked me if I was going to tell Doug about the sexual abuse. My response was, "No way. There's no way I can do that."

I had an assignment in my workbook that asked me what steps I was going to take next in order to get support from friends and family as I deal with the crisis. I wrote: I need to find a way to tell Doug.

I'll never be able to do that. No chance. There's no way in hell. If I think he doesn't relate to me now, how much will he accept me after I tell him something whacked out like that?

I completed another exercise where I outlined what I would need to do to take care of myself as I worked through my problems. Then, I had to define the worst case scenarios and how they would impact me. For instance, if I couldn't handle the stress, then I wrote that I could potentially lose my job, lose my house, lose my husband, lose my friends. And I realized that at that point, nothing mattered except for the way I felt. I wanted to fix myself at any cost.

On my next visit, we talked about how important it is to tell about what happened in order to heal.

I don't want people to know this sh* about me! It's nasty! Why do I have to tell anyone? It's not my fault! It has nothing to do with me now, anyway! It's old stuff. Can't we just forget about it? How do I make it go away? It's been like thirty years! I've moved on. Why does it matter!

The next two weeks, I was crippled by my own memories. I was in complete crisis – admitting to myself for the first time what had really happened – the details, getting professional help, and at the same time trying to figure out why I was insistent that my marriage needed to end. I decided that either I was going to stay with him and be wide open, or I was going to leave.

What do I have to lose? Right now we have zero. If I scare him away, my decision is made.

I called him on my way home from work. Just as I hoped he would, he asked how my lunchtime therapy appointment went. "It was good," I said.

I'm going to tell him. I need him to understand me.

"We talked about things that I've never talked about before," I said.

"Yeah? Like what?" he asked.

"This is horrible. It's embarrassing."

I can't do it.

"That's okay. You can tell me," he assured me.

I was in the long line of traffic from Sunrise Valley turning right on Frying Pan road. Cars were pushing their way into the turn lane, anxious to get past the Frying Pan mess and onto 28.

The tears started. Not just a few tears. Big tears. "I was sexually abused when I was a kid," I blurted out. My head was exploding.

Oh crap. What am I feeling?

"Oh my gosh, you were?" he asked, compassionately.

"Yes." I started crying harder than ever before.

I feel so sad right now.

"Oh honey, I'm so sorry. By who?"

He sounded angry at whoever it might be.

I can't answer this. I can't talk about it. What is he thinking right now?

"My Uncle Louis, and actually my grandfather – my mom's dad, but he's dead."

I began sobbing uncontrollably and gave him a few bits of information about when and where, and so on. I told him how I was always scared of being attacked and how I would fight them off.

"Gina, that's terrible. No one deserves to go through that. I'm going to help you. I love you. I'm so sorry."

"I think this is a lot of the reason why we're having so many problems," I sobbed.

I'm talking out loud here. What am I saying? What does this have to do with our marriage?

"Even though I feel like you don't talk to me on a deeper level, the reality is that I don't talk to you. I have been keeping in this horrible secret, and I've been too scared to talk to you or anyone else about it until I told Dr. Young."

"Which grandfather was it? Is it the one in that picture in the living room?"

Uh oh, he thinks badly of me for having that picture.

"Yes, he's in that picture. But I'm too afraid to take it down because then my parents might ask questions that I won't want to answer. He's dead anyway."

"What about the uncle? Which one is it?"

He sounds so protective and caring.

I explained which one, but he wasn't sure. I have so many relatives on my mom's side. "You know the aunt you always say looks mean? It's her husband," I explained.

I went home, and we talked, and I cried, and we hugged. I was just beginning the crisis stage of acknowledging my abuse, and at the same time Doug and I were starting to address our damaged marriage. So much had happened in just one week.

Records from subsequent therapy sessions read: Patient took a huge risk and told her husband about the past sexual abuse. Was surprised by his total support, feels now much closer to him, reconnected.

Explored patterns of workaholic in self as she feels safe by doing. Patient fears relaxing as feelings that are difficult may come up. Difficulties being in the moment. Anxiety leads to constantly planning for the future. Also patterns of hyper vigilance. This worked for her in advancing her career, yet put her in defensive mode. Making connections between patterns of "doing" rather than "being" and avoiding pain of abuse.

Will start exploring what and how it feels for patient to try and experience her feelings here with me.

Patient indicated that since mother confronted uncle about his sexual abuse of patient, the secret is out of the bag. A cousin came out and disclosed her abuse by him. Now patient also concerned about her brother who is rather fragile. Much inner turmoil. Processing feelings of sadness and "unhappiness" with marriage. To stay or leave?

Processing feelings of ambivalence and tension relating to marriage and past sexual abuse.

Patient is rather upset and agitated.

Worked on self esteem, self concept as patient overly concerned about what others think of her and tends to take on personally others' projected judgments. Self esteem work.

For over eight months I had been cold and distant from Doug. All I wanted was for him to leave me. I wanted to be alone and be deep with my thoughts. I told myself that he kept me from being creative, intimate, passionate. It was all his fault, I was sure.

Yet, I read and went to therapy because of the overwhelming doubt in myself. Although I felt strongly that this was a stay or go decision, I didn't trust my own perceptions. I would make a list of reasons to stay and reasons to go, and nothing was compelling. I was confused and unable to focus.

Doug thought that the therapy was a good thing, and he assured me that he would support me through the decision. He'd come and sit down with me and say things like, "I'm not just letting you go that easily. I'm not letting you throw this all away. I'll give you as much time as you need to figure it out."

Everybody has monsters in their basement. That's what Dr. Young says. You have to invite the monsters up to your living room once in a while, and let them spend time with you. No one wants to do that... the monsters are dirty. They're not nice, and they're not pretty. But if you don't invite them, then they'll just pop up when you least expect them, and when you least want them to.

My monsters are all over my living room right now. It's like a scary monster frat party.

I decided to show Doug the chapter in my book that is written for husbands, partners, and boyfriends of women survivors of childhood sexual abuse. Right then and there, he sat down and read the whole thing.

I can't believe he's reading all that. He hates reading.

"This explains so much about you, you know, Gina? Now I understand why you are the way you are." He came over and held me. In that moment, I felt like we had the most genuine connection of the ten years since we met. I was understood. I was accepted.

I don't love myself. I hate what I've been doing to him. He deserves better.

Months of emotional meltdown followed. I was exhausted. I made my way to work barely able to focus. People asked me what was wrong. "I had a rough night," I'd say. And they would laugh, thinking I was out drinking. I'd smile, and they had no idea.

I was on Route 50 near Chantilly, and the traffic was guaranteeing me another half hour of stop and go between there and 66. I found myself silently reciting the string of profanities that I said over and over to myself, uncontrollably, as a kid.

Little shitty f***ing son of a bitchy bastard hell of a jackass son of a whore. Stop it. Little shitty f***ing son of a bitchy bastard hell of a jackass son of a whore.

At first it was hole, then, once I had learned the word whore, I thought that made more sense, so I switched it.

Why can't I stop saying this? I don't want to say this anymore. Why do I even think it? Who says these awful things?! Where did I learn these words? I need to bring this up with Dr. Young and see what she has to say. But I'm too embarrassed to tell her. She'll think I'm a freak. I can't stop swearing. It's horrible!

I've wondered about that bad language thing ever since I can remember. I certainly didn't learn those words at home. Not in our Christian home where everything was perfect – all kindness, all loving, all peaceful and caring.

It was first grade when I was behind Dorset School near the hockey rink, and I shouted it out at my brother and laughed. I was mad at him for something, most likely out of embarrassment. He told my mom, and she asked where I learned those words.

"I don't know," I said.

"You probably heard it from the big kids at school," she assured me.

I didn't agree, but I nodded anyway. I didn't remember where I learned it, but it was a long time ago, of that I was sure.

She proceeded to caution me about how inappropriate it is to use those words. Then, she told me what each of them really meant, and I was even more ashamed that this phrase had already circled in and out of my thoughts thousands of times.

Here I was, thirty years later, swearing to myself again on my way home from work and thinking about kneeling on the blue living room carpet and leaning against the cold marble and walnut coffee table while my mom explained to me what I was saying. I couldn't stop dwelling on the words.

My New Year's resolution for 2006 had been to stop using bad language, and that was probably the twenty-fifth time I had attempted to quit cursing. Again, I failed.

In the evenings, I'd lie in bed with Doug, and he would come over to kiss me, which I always loved. But with these fresh memories, any initiation of kissing made me feel like I was four years old with my uncle trying to lick me all over my lips, squeeze my breasts, tickle my private parts and make me touch him. I knew it was just memories creeping in, and I'd try to ignore them. But I could see his face, the glasses, the greasy hair, his gross French accent. I could see him. I panicked. My heart would race, and I felt the fear of the abuse as if it was happening now.

Vivid flashbacks. The nasty polyester pants. Green ones, brown ones, navy blue, grey. The shirts. Short-sleeved, light blue or white with a black leather eyeglass case in his pocket. How he touched me, grabbed me, shoving his hands inside my clothes every chance he could get to rub, squeeze, and penetrate. His heavy body against my small frame, holding me down and smothering me with nastiness. The shape of his small tight lips and that stupid tongue he would never keep to himself. The chirping bird in his kitchen that he loved so much. How he would attack and kiss me as if I was his lover, and how I tried so hard to push him away and fight him off.

The dog. That big huge dog named Kelly whose slobber reminded me of my uncle. Messy, dirty, and dripping saliva, and so big that I couldn't get out from under him. The smell of the dirt in my uncle's front yard, and the rocks that they paid my brother and I to clean up.

Hot dogs and homemade French fries, everything fried. His fat stomach and how he would point mine out after dinner and laugh, "Regarde la grosse bedaine!" (Look at your big fat belly!)

I'd explain that I was having disturbing flashbacks to Doug, and he would hold me. With trust and talking, the flashbacks would pass. But it was confusing and painful, not to mention annoying and disruptive to our intimacy, which I cherished.

I just want to live my life and forget about all of this. I love my husband. I want my life back. I want my relationship with Doug back.

I kept thinking about ways to get revenge. I imagined what I would do if I saw that asshole Uncle, and I told my therapist about it. I wrote about it. I seriously considered taking some type of action.

I should just go up there.

I knew that if I acted on my thoughts, I would end up going to jail.

I was furious. Furious. For the first time in my life, I understood the desire and hunger for revenge and the difficulty of not taking action. I was uncomfortable with my anger. I wanted to blow his head off. I wanted him to suffer. I wanted him to feel terror, pain, agony, fear, and confusion. And, I wanted him to never know when it would end. I wanted to watch him suffer.

I went through my workbook section by section, writing about what had happened to me, how I coped, what behaviors I had adopted in response to the abuse. I finally understood why I do the things I do, why I'm so picky, why I can't live in chaos and disorder, why I have certain likes and dislikes, why I feel the way I feel, and why I've lived the way I've lived. I've always hated myself, always thought I was

ugly, always gotten in trouble for acting out, always gone after
the opposite of what was good for me.

*I'm always in search of escape. When I see a broken
person on the streets, I can relate. I picture myself sitting on a
cold, hard, dirty floor, leaning against a wall, unable to cry. I
want to walk nowhere forever and feel the woods and the cold,
the wind and the sky. To stare at the earth so intently that I
become a part of it. And fade into nothingness.*

I felt so uncomfortable at my high school graduation
that I wore sunglasses the entire time and left the instant the
ceremony was over. I wore only black for 3 years straight in
college. I shaved checkers into the back of my head. I changed
my hair color and cut every month because I never looked
good. I pierced my own nose at a bar. I drank until I threw up.
I gained and lost weight twice a year from fluctuating
depression, anxiety and stress – 30 pounds up, then 40 pounds
down, then 25, then 20. I was always miserable about being
who I was, and every year I was ashamed and embarrassed of
the previous year. I wanted to change and move on from
everything all the time. I didn't want to run into people I
knew, because I was always embarrassed about the person I
had been and the way I looked.

All of this understanding was like pouring anger all
over me. I was pissed. All of these things that I hated about

myself had evolved from the abuse and the denial. I cried, I read, I wrote, I talked openly to Doug, I spaced out, I spent a lot of time in Dr. Young's blue chair, and I worked through the crisis. Doug held me, reassured me, loved me and supported me.

The crisis lasted for about 6 months, and it was like getting to know each other all over again. I was finally open, and we were talking. I expressed how I felt and how much it scared me. Although I'm sure he was nervous about what I was saying, he stood by me like a soldier. Never questioning intentions, always ready to support me.

We sat on the couch, and every night I was a complete mess. I was broken. I was sorry. I was angry. I was sad. And, Doug was right there with me. He didn't make it go away, but he was right there with me, and he still loved me.

Doug made me feel truly safe for the first time in my life.

"Gina, you're such a good person. You've taught me so much about real love, and you've shown me what it's like to have a real relationship. We're a good team. We bring out the best in each other and always help other people. You're generous and thoughtful, and you've taught me to be the same. You'll be okay. You have so much to live for. I'm here for you. I want you here with me."

Work had been driving me crazy. While I was crumbling inside, I was succeeding in business better than ever. But, I knew that I wasn't being compensated equally to my peers, despite performing the same activities and bringing in even better results in some cases. I sought out an executive coach through my business network and had my first appointment on August 1.

Bethany Gray was an exceptional woman, experienced in both mentoring and operating in the business world. She began the session by telling me a little about her qualifications and other clients and asked me to give her some background so that we could set goals for our coaching relationship.

I described my role at work and explained some of the political and organizational challenges, emphasizing that I felt as though my leadership took advantage of me and that I was treated unfairly.

Bethany encouraged me to expand on my story to include other aspects of my life, and I matter-of-factly admitted that I was currently undergoing therapy for childhood sexual abuse and that that was going well.

You're only the third person I've ever told, aside from my husband and my therapist.

"Oh, Gina," she said caringly, "you wouldn't believe how often I hear that from my clients and those of my colleagues. So many are very successful people like you. It's amazing how common it is these days to run across people who are working through the long-term effects of abuse. You are not alone."

"Really?" I asked.

"Really. I'm glad you're getting help. That's so important. It just doesn't make sense to try to tackle career-related issues without addressing challenges that are so much deeper. You know, so much of who you are is based on the story that you tell yourself, and that includes how you describe your childhood, your best and worst moments, and who you are today."

"Hmm. Well, I think I'm doing pretty well with therapy, but I still have a long way to go." A single tear made its way out of the corner of my left eye, and I quickly wiped it away.

"That's great," she said, with an encouraging touch on my shoulder.

Bethany and I went through an in-depth evaluation of my values, personality type, life experiences, interpretations and thoughts, what has strengthened me and what has made me weaker.

My initial workbook notes focused on areas at work where I was fearful, a victim, tired, and not valued. I developed a plan for re-establishing myself in a healthier and more supportive environment. Within two weeks, I outlined what I wanted from my current employer, including equal pay and a promotion to reflect the work I was doing. I also put together an alternate plan for pursuing work at another company in case my firm wasn't willing to grant my requests.

All I had to do was ask, and I got what I requested.

"You're right, Bethany," I said, "All I had to do was explain my value and what I deserved, and they immediately agreed to make the changes."

"That's right," she replied. "You're worth it!"

T he letter arrived by registered mail Canada Post, postmarked August 28, 2006. It was a chaotic looking envelope, having been typed in huge font.

Look at his return address. Eww. There's a f*ing bird on it. And why isn't my aunt's name on there as well?

I left it on the counter for 3 days, until I was emotionally ready to read it.

The letter, in somewhat broken English, said:

"Gina Lynn,"

Dumb ass. My middle name has one 'n' – not two. And who calls me that anyway?

"After meeting with your mother on the week end, she told me that you are suffering a lot about things I have done to you when you were young."

Yeah, she told me she was going to confront you at the family reunion.

"When I asked her what it was, she said she didn't know."

What?!

"But Monday morning, she remembered and said it to your aunt Ginger and possibly the other ones, but that is not the point."

You're right it's not the point, and what do you mean my mom didn't know what it was? You're such a liar! So did my aunt Ginger approach you? What are you trying to say here anyway?

"I want to ask your forgiveness for what I had done to you, I know that you where deeply marked by my actions, I also know that even if I ask you to forgive me and forget, it is very hard for you. The marks will be in your memory for a long time. When we plant a nail, it makes a mark that stays there even if we remove the nail. The same thing happens when there is something wrong in our heart."

Oh my gosh, what is this crap! He is trying to give a sermon.

"I asked the Lord to forgive me about that a long time ago, and I never tough about asking you, to forgive me, and I completely forgot these event after that, but I never thought about reaching you to ask you for your pardon."

You forgot?! Bullsh*. What about the others? Did you forget about them? Do you expect anyone to believe that I was the only one? And you never thought about reaching me to ask for my pardon? Hmm, sounds to me like you really only cared about yourself.

"I saw you a few times after you moved to the state but, for me, it was forgiven by the Lord so I forgot all about it. I should have think to ask you to pardon me, but, I am sorry I did not."

Yes, I'm sure it was devastating when I moved away so that you couldn't have me as your little girlfriend anymore. And, when I saw you those few times, you made sure to throw some inappropriate comments my way. I see right through you, you complete jerk.

"Now it might be too late, I hope not, I know the Lord still hear me, and that He could help you with that problem. I am sorry also for your parents and I did asked them to forgive me Saturday night, they said it was OK, but I am not sure that they will forget."

I'm sure my parents didn't say it was okay.

"Also, I am sorry for my beloved wife, I know she is suffering a lot from that and it is only starting, because of me."

Oh, here we go! Start worrying about yourself!

"She mention to me this morning that she is really worried for the future, I am the guilty one, she should not suffer for that."

Of course you're worried about your wife, because she takes care of you, and you would be lost without her. I would be willing to bet that the only reason you wrote this letter is so that you could show her that you wrote it. And I notice that this lovely paragraph about your beloved wife is in bold... because you are so sorry for the rift you have caused in your marriage. Who is the letter to – her or me?

"I really do not know what to say, to make you feel good, but I just hope you will accept my request for forgiveness. You can be sure you will never hear from me except if you ask for it, but I am sure you are not interested in that, and I understand your feelings for revenge, if you think that could help you."

What does this mean? Do you want me to take revenge?

"On my side, I feel like I should disappear, get out of everybody's life but it is in your hands."

Drama. You disappearing is in my hands? Should I wave my magic wand?

"On your side, try to figure out I never existed, consider me as dead, that way it might be easier to forget me."

No sh*, Sherlock. If I could forget that you ever existed, my life would be perfect.

"I am sorry that I was a nightmare in your life rather than being a blessing. Gina, I am really sincere in my request, hope you will consider it and forgive, and try to forget."

The only thing you're sincere about is yourself and how much you want everyone to feel sorry for you.

"You know, your life is surely not easy, and it is because of me. But mine is not any better, I have to live with guilt for as long as I know you are in trouble and for the rest of my life, and this is my fault."

Good, feel guilty, please. If this letter is about you, write it to yourself.

"Gina,"

Stop saying my f*ing name!

"I am not sure I used the right words for this letter, you know I am doing my best to write in English. God Bless you Gina."

You're disgusting.

"Louis."

Puke. I hate you. You ruined my childhood.

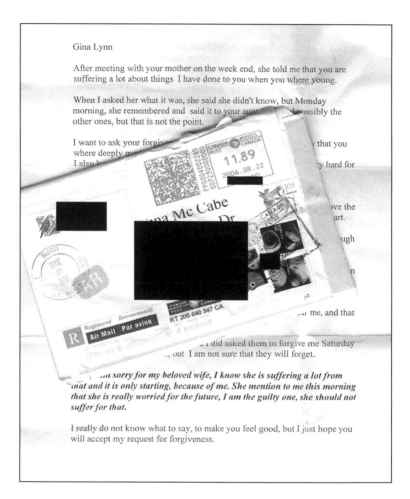

Gina Lynn

After meeting with your mother on the week end, she told me that you are suffering a lot about things I have done to you when you where young.

When I asked her what it was, she said she didn't know, but Monday morning, she remembered and said it to your aunt possibly the other ones, but that is not the point.

I want to ask your forgive... ...y that you where deeply m... I also k... ...y hard for

...ve the ...art.

...ugh

...n

...u me, and that

...i did asked them to forgive me Saturday ..., out I am not sure that they will forget.

...m sorry for my beloved wife, I know she is suffering a lot from that and it is only starting, because of me. She mention to me this morning that she is really worried for the future, I am the guilty one, she should not suffer for that.

I really do not know what to say, to make you feel good, but I just hope you will accept my request for forgiveness.

It took me a week or so to process what I had read, and it took a month and a lot of courage to write back. When I read what I wrote now, it seems very unemotional and practical; that's a reflection of how I had become.

Here's the email I sent him:

Louis,

I'm writing to you once, and I only want ONE email back with exactly the information I'm requesting at the end of this email. Beyond that, do not write to me unless I send you an email requesting a response.

I cringed just to see that you typed my name, as you don't deserve to even be able to say it.

Did you really need to hear from my mother that I've been suffering a lot about the things that you did to me when I was a child? Let's see, if I remember correctly it was as young as age 2 or 3. Does it get any sicker than that? Are you that much in denial of what a controlling, manipulative, disgusting and selfish person you have been and still are?

In your letter, you said that you want to ask for forgiveness. Then, you said that:

1) you never thought about asking me to forgive you

2) you completely forgot these events after that, and

3) for you, it was forgiven by the Lord.

Well, guess what? It's not that easy, and I think you are full of crap.

First of all, for you to hide in religion makes me sick. Secondly, if you think God forgives you when you don't even feel remorse, you should think again. If you think asking God for forgiveness was more important than asking me, you're wrong.

You have been so bold. You have always taken every possible opportunity to try to say inappropriate things to me, both when I was a child and every single time I have seen you since. The fact that you continually calling me "Ma Blonde" didn't raise any red flags with the family surprises me.

You caused me tremendous confusion because you were my uncle, someone who is supposed to love me and be trustworthy, yet you were a predator who constantly tried to molest me for your own gain. You also caused me sheer terror and put me in a continual state of alertness, trying to hide or run away whenever you came near.

I remember staying over at your house and lying awake terrified that you were going to come in my room and try to kiss me, touch me, molest me. I was too young to understand my fear and the confusion. All I knew was that I was supposed to love you and have fun with you but that I hated whenever you physically came near me. It made me feel so scared, unsafe, unprotected, vulnerable, and alone, and I was unable to communicate the problem because I was too young, too confused, and too afraid.

Even though I wasn't able to process what was really going on, I always, always pushed you away. You knew very well that I didn't like you coming near me, yet you dismissed my needs and tried to playfully ease closer and closer. I remember your boldness, when we sat as an extended family in my parents' dining room, you next to me at a formal dinner, and you reached under the table and up my dress to grope me all over my private areas right there at the same table with your wife and my family. You didn't care about anyone but yourself and whatever sick desire for control or sexuality that you were feeding.

You are so misled if you think that you can hide in the church and any religion. Who else did you molest? Nadia? Luc? Anne-Marie? Mike? Who are you messing with today? What websites do you visit online? Child pornography? Do you try to have adult conversations with young kids? Do you use inappropriate language and try to get kids to talk about sex for your pleasure? Research shows that in order for a molester to be caught ONCE, they have already molested over ONE HUNDRED kids. I remember when Viviane told the aunts that you had tried to kiss her. So, you've been caught more than once. You are a sick person, and it's time to admit that you need more help.

Here's what I need you to do. First, I need you to send me a list of all children that you've ever even TRIED to kiss or touch like an adult or molested or abused in any way – verbally, physically or sexually. That way, I can at LEAST reach out to them, and we can support each other in dealing with the devastating after-effects of your abuse. Second, I need you to send me a list of any cohorts you previously had or have today, so that we are all aware of other family members (whether your family or ours), friends, and/or co-workers who have also been child molesters or abusers in ANY way – whether past or present. If you have friends who are into child porn, it's time to let us know. And, you know exactly what I'm talking about, so don't pretend that you don't. You are obviously in denial, so it's time to bring things back to the front of your mind. Who else may have previously caused some damage within your family or ours? Who else is interested in sexual acts with children like you are? Who else was aware of what you were doing when we were children? We need to create awareness so that others can be kept safe and can deal with the suffering. I already know some of this, and if you lie to me, you are asking for trouble. I'm giving you ONE CHANCE to be 100% honest in all of the information that you provide.

My concerns are:

1) My healing

2) Healing of my other family members, cousins, etc who went through similar suffering

3) Knowing that everyone is aware of any other people who you know have been abusers or contributors either in the past or present.

Send me the lists right away. I want to talk to my brother and cousins and anyone else who might need help. And, I want to let everyone know what other adults you know were ever child predators.

What a jerk. I was so small... just like little Leah! I don't understand how anyone can do something so disturbing

*to an innocent, trusting, loving little child. First of all, how did
he get this urge? Secondly, how did he act on it, knowing that
it would so clearly be harmful? Does he not realize that he
needs help? If he was abused, then doesn't he know how
painful it was? Why on earth would he want to pass that
humiliation on to someone else?*

*Wow. Remember that time when Leah was at our
house, and she ran out of the bathroom without her clothes on,
laughing? I panicked! "Leah, please go back in there and put
your clothes on," I said. She did. Right away. I was wondering
– what if her parents came to the door?! What if they thought I
was being inappropriate with her? I would never! I began to
have another memory of my uncle that day, but I didn't let it
come.*

*When Leah returned properly dressed, we went
outside. I told her parents what had happened. They laughed
and joked about how she likes to run around naked. I was
surprised at how uncomfortable I was in the situation. I had
not come to terms with my own abuse, yet I just knew that I
refused to be even remotely associated with anything that
could be perceived as inappropriate behavior with a child.*

*What about that time at my cousin's house. I think I
was five or six. My cousin's room and her parents' bedroom
were right across the hall from each other. When I came out*

*after changing into my play clothes, there stood my aunt –
buck naked, folding some laundry in her room with the door
wide open. I immediately turned away and went into the
bathroom.*

*When forever was up, I came back outside, and she
was still there, still working on laundry, still nude.*

*"What?" she asked with a smile, "Doesn't your
mother walk around the house naked?" She laughed and took
a sip of her coffee.*

*"No," I said, embarrassed for both her and me, and I
ran outside to find my cousins.*

That was, and still is, so weird.

*What about that discussion I had with mom when I
told her about Uncle Louis. And her first question was, "Oh
no, was there any rape?" Who the f* cares if there was rape,
oral sex, fondling, pornography, squeezing, licking! What the
hell difference does it make?! It was f*ing disturbing! It was
inappropriate! It was horrible. There's no level of detail that
makes it okay or NOT okay. It's NOT okay. Period. It's
repulsive, dreadful and horrifying. The specifics are
irrelevant, and nothing minimizes it, nor does anything make it
so much worse. It just sucks.*

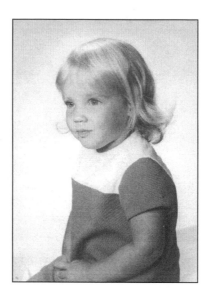

Y ou never know how traffic will be in Arlington, so I was a few minutes early to the restaurant. I stopped into Macy's and bought yet another lipstick that I didn't need and probably wouldn't wear. When I'm about to buy makeup, I think about how much better I could potentially look, and then when I try to wear it, it's either too bright, too pale, too noticeable, or the wrong color for my skin tone. No matter what, when I look in the mirror, I never think I look good. Nevertheless, for the hundredth time, I bought the lipstick, certain that it would make me look better.

The restaurant was right next door. I was shown to a table and asked if I could instead be seated at the cozier looking booth. I could see the door from there, and it seemed much more private.

There he is. He still looks the same!

"Heyyyyyy." We hugged. "Good to see you."

"You too!" We sat down.

"This is a cool place," I said.

"Yeah, Dana and I come here once in a while, and it's right around the corner from work."

"It's been years since I've seen you."

"I know. Your skin looks great."

That is such a Sam thing to say.

"It's good makeup," I smiled.

Check the lipstick, check the lipstick.

"Check the lipstick!" I said, unable to not point it out.

"Sweet, girlfriend!"

We talked for a while, he caught me up on his fiancée Dana and their upcoming wedding, I told him about Doug, we talked about our careers and reminisced about when we used to work together at TGI Fridays during college.

"So, I guess you're wondering why I reached out to you after all of these years," I asked.

"Yeah, you tryin' to sell me some Amway or something?"

"Ha ha ha. I wish I was," I replied, and tried to put myself together. "This is awkward, okay, and I don't even know if you remember this. But, do you remember, one afternoon, you and I were grabbing lunch in between shifts, and you told me this story about how your babysitter or someone like that had sexually molested or raped you repeatedly when you were a kid? Do you remember telling me that?"

"Uhh, I don't remember telling you." He paused. "But it is true. He was a neighbor, actually. Where were we?"

"American Café, I think, in Tysons."

"Huh. Nope. Don't remember. Anyway, what about it?"

"Okay, well I remember that, when you told me, I felt really upset with what I was hearing, and I was like 'why is he telling me this?!' What I'm trying to say is that I was really unsupportive of you when you needed a friend, and I wanted to apologize to you for that and see how you're doing. I realize it's been a ridiculously long time, but I've been thinking about that recently, and I feel awful."

"Gina, I don't even remember that. I appreciate you saying something, but obviously it didn't affect me negatively. What the hell made you think of all of this?"

"I'm in therapy right now, because I was sexually abused as a child as well."

"Really."

"Yeah. It sucks. And in the work that I've been doing to deal with it, I've realized that so much of my behavior is a result of my abuse. When you told me about the horrible things that happened to you, I wanted to shut you out. I couldn't stand to hear it, because I had never faced what had happened to me. I was struggling to keep it all pushed down, and your story was bringing it to the surface. I've always felt gross, embarrassed and ashamed when I hear of any type of rape or sexual abuse – almost guilty. It doesn't make sense logically, but it's an overwhelming feeling. It's like I couldn't bear to hear or deal with your story. Today, I understand why, and I just wanted to let you know."

"Wow. So, do you want to talk about what happened to you?"

I laughed. "Not really!"

"Okay that's fine." He smiled, "So what happened?"

"Uh. It was my uncle. When I was like a toddler."

"God."

"Yeah, asshole."

"And so how's the therapy going?"

"It's helping. You're like the third or fourth person I've told now. I'm getting better at it. But I don't understand why I feel so gross about it all? Why do I feel horrible? Do you feel that way?"

"I used to. But, you know what? There's a light at the end of the tunnel."

"Really?" I believed him.

That's a relief.

"Really," he assured me.

"Not a day goes by when I don't have flashbacks or think about it at least ten times, and it gives me shivers. It makes me sick. It interferes with my life and my work. I hate it. I can't stop my brain. And, I have terrible anxiety."

"I used to have all that. But I don't have it anymore. In fact, I've gone probably more than two years now without it ever crossing my mind."

I laughed nervously and covered my mouth, "Oh great, and I made you bring it up again!"

"No, it's fine," he said.

"You really never think about it?"

"Rarely. You'll get better. It just takes time."

"That's encouraging."

That's hard to believe. But, God, I hope it's true.

We talked more about the upcoming wedding, about his love of travel and partying, and people we used to know. Normal stuff with old friends. It was good to see him, but more than anything I was glad to have checked the box on this item of guilt. I still had another box to check with Cole, but that would be a much bigger step since we had so many mutual friends who had no idea about my issues.

Sam and I hugged, promised not to wait so long in between seeing each other again, and parted ways. I thought about the discussion the whole way back to work.

I sat down and covered myself with one of the pillows, got my water bottle ready and took a deep breath.

"So, what's going on?" asked Dr. Young.

"Lots of good stuff," I said.

"Tell me," she grinned.

"Remember the old friend I told you about, Sam, who had confided in me about his abuse – the one I felt guilty about for not being supportive?"

"Yes, I do."

"I had lunch with him on Friday and apologized."

"And what was his reaction?"

"He was so great about it; in fact, he never even recalled that I was anything but supportive. I feel a lot better now. He also made it seem like there's hope for me."

"You took a big step, didn't you?"

"Yes."

"Good for you."

"And, actually, I also wrote my uncle back on Sunday," I smiled. "It was a really rough weekend for me, and I decided that I just needed to tell him how I felt."

"You did? Good for you!"

"Yes, I brought my email along. Want me to read it to you?" I was trying not to allow myself to feel too proud.

"Sure."

I proceeded to read it, and then I explained that he had not responded to my email yet.

"Do you expect that he really will answer you?"

"Yes, I hope so!"

I'm really hoping that he will. You don't think he will?

"What if he never does?"

I never even considered that. You really don't think he'll write me back? I'm expecting an email response with exactly the information I requested.

"It will be okay," I admitted. "But I might keep sending him emails or calling him non-stop until he does," I said, with a smirk.

"Okay," she smiled back.

"Before coming here today, I was sure that he would reply. I really want to know who else he abused. And, I want to know who else in the family was in on the whole thing. I think there are more secrets."

"Tell me more about why you think that."

"It's hard to remember; it was so long ago. But I can remember him and my grandfather being in the whole thing together. Like, at my grandparents' farm, the whole family would be there, and I was just a toddler. And my grandfather would pick me up and put me on his lap, and he would try to touch me inappropriately."

It is so hard to talk about this. It makes me feel disgusting.

"Inappropriately, how so?"

"It's gross," I said.

"That's okay."

"He would, like, try to jam his fingers up inside me, inside my clothes, while I was sitting on his lap. I mean, both in the front and the back."

Eww gross! I'm shivering.

"And I would be wiggling to get away, but he would clutch onto me tightly, and I felt scared and didn't know what to do. He had me convinced that nothing was going on. Then, this one time, as if it was a game, he handed me over to my uncle, and he did the same thing. I distinctly remember them smiling at each other as if they were in on the secret. I felt like I was imagining that it was happening, and I would always get away as soon as I could, but it was hard to push away without attracting attention as to what was happening. I was always trying to escape them. Yet, as if it wasn't confusing enough, I loved them both."

And today I hate them. And more than anything, I hate the secrets. I hate that people didn't notice. I hated family gatherings. I hated being chased. I hated being afraid.

"So, I wonder, if my grandfather did this to me, then who else did he do it to? He had, like, nine kids, and six of them were girls. My mom left home when she was just twelve or thirteen, I think. I asked her why she left, and she says that it was only because she had an opportunity to move in with a family where she could have a good education and learn English. I thought that was weird. What young teen would want to leave their parents and their family for an education, unless something was really wrong at home? She says her father beat up her and her siblings but that everyone did that in those days and that there was never anything sexual. I'm just not sure I buy the whole thing. I bet there are things she doesn't know."

"I also remember hearing about some weird phone sex thing involving my grandfather, a different uncle, and the wife of another uncle who had died. One of my aunts called my mom and told her about this strange behavior on the part of my grandfather, and my mom asked me, 'Can you believe grandpapa would be involved in something like that?' and, of course, I assured her that he wouldn't do anything like that."

"This week, I asked my mom about that story again, and she says she doesn't remember it. She explained that as my grandfather's brain tumor grew, he demonstrated all sorts of disturbing behavior and that perhaps that was the explanation. I don't know. There are just too many secrets in the family."

Dr. Young wrapped up the session with a thought-provoking illustration, as she did many times.

"Life is like a river that flows through you," she said, "and all of this bad stuff is like sticks and trash that blocks the flow of the water. Every once in a while, you have to reach in and pick out the trash. You have to clear the branches so that the water can flow again. It's hard work. But when the river is flowing, you experience life."

D r. Young's records from our subsequent therapy sessions highlighted the challenges I was facing:

Patient experienced a big melt down this weekend. Worked more with the workbook, "Courage to Heal." Crying for two days straight. Feelings of despair, pain, anger. Wrote letter to her abuser. Angry with his wife, too (her aunt). Deep processing.

Patient is shifting some of her feelings and attitudes related to her marriage. She's owning up to her part and exploring the projections she has been making.

As she is continuing work, more fresh memories of abuse surface, processed. Also exploring her tendency to put a mask on.

Issues with mother and family dynamics. Anger for not being seen or acknowledged as a person at times, by mom, by uncle and grandfather.

Patient indicated she would like to take a break from therapy. Seems flooded by potential intensity of experience of memories, flashbacks and feelings and potential plans of action. Seems like a break may work well for now. Much more work to be done in terms of meeting treatment plan.

It was the night before my fourth career coaching session with Bethany. I was preparing notes on what career-related issues I wanted to discuss with her. This time I was supposed to focus on what brings me joy, since every evaluation tool showed that my happiness score was low.

In my coaching journal, I wrote:

I'm realizing that it's been years since I've really spent a lot of time doing things that make me happy – music, art, writing, baking, spending time with friends. Instead, I've been spending all of my energy setting and reaching goals, and getting to the next level at work. I haven't been enjoying life. Maybe I need to step back and relax, balance more, do the things that I really love, in order to be happier. Moving forward to me has always meant reaching academic, professional or relationship goals. Today, maybe moving forward means actively pursuing what makes me happy and enjoying life more. I could let my career progress naturally.

"This is a big step, Gina," Bethany said when we met the next afternoon. "You're changing your entire outlook on your career."

"Yes! I mean, why should I be chasing and rushing and pushing for more instead of living. I think it's time to slow down."

Bethany was so supportive. We continued meeting and discussed how things were going, how I was feeling, and we continually re-evaluated how I could enjoy myself more on a day to day basis at work.

D oug and I were scurrying around the kitchen making ourselves some hot tea.

"My mom is going to have Thanksgiving at her house this year, and she wants you to invite your parents, too" Doug said.

My face dropped.

Sh*. I don't wanna go. This gets me every time. The holidays stress me out so much. Every year it's the same daunting feeling. Can't we just cancel the holidays?

"Okay," I mumbled.

He knew better.

"Honey, what is wrong?" he asked. "It's just a family get-together."

"It's just — I hate holidays. I don't like big gatherings. You don't understand how nervous it makes me. I'm so self-conscious, and I have trouble doing the small talk thing." I felt myself get shaky.

"That's okay," he said, "It's our family. We all love you." He came over and hugged me.

"No, that's not it. When I was young, holidays and family get-togethers were where I was attacked and abused." I covered my face with my hands and started to cry. "I hated it! You know how upset I get when we go to your family's house and you leave me alone to go hang out with your cousins or whatever? It's because I feel scared and vulnerable being alone.

Even though I'm an adult and I know nothing is going to happen, I can't help the feelings," I sobbed. "I'm thirty-six, but the holidays make me feel like I'm three, and being at large gatherings without you right by my side makes me feel vulnerable. I know my fears are unrealistic, but I feel the fear as if the danger is really there."

I don't want to go! I'm scared.

He hugged me closer and gently pushed my hair back from my face. "I'm sorry. I love you so much. We don't even have to go. We never have to go. I'll just tell them we're not coming, and everything will be fine."

"Really?" I asked.

Did he just say that we don't have to go?

"Really. It's not that important. I want you to feel okay. You're the most important thing in the world to me."

Oh my gosh. That is so nice. What a relief!

"Oh, thank you so much. That makes me feel so much better."

I cried more, and we talked about the different scenarios that throw me back in time and flood me with fear.

"I'll call my mom," he said, "and tell her that we're not coming. It's no big deal."

Later that day, I decided that we could go.

And, we went. And it was fine. It wasn't the best day ever, but it was much better than it had ever been before. I wasn't scared, and I didn't feel so out of place. Doug stayed by my side most of the time, and he would ask if it was okay if he went for a few minutes to shoot hoops outside or play video games with his cousins. He knew I was afraid. He checked on me often, without it being weird. I was okay.

By the next few family gatherings, I still felt stressed in advance, but I felt safer because I knew that he knew. I didn't need him by my side anymore, and I wasn't afraid.

Just telling him helped everything become less intimidating.

Now that my dad had been diagnosed with Shy-Drager Syndrome, with symptoms progressing rapidly, my parents decided to plan a family vacation in the Outer Banks. They picked the nicest beach house available where we could all relax and spend time together.

We stayed at Ocean Waves, a gorgeous oceanfront home in Duck. It was Doug and me, my parents, and my brother Mike and his wife and son.

Wednesday morning I slept in until 9 a.m., and when I peeked out to see what the weather was doing, I saw my mom and Mike sitting out on the private beach access deck. She looked at him, and he at her. Then, they looked away, and each took turns wiping their eyes.

Why are they crying?

"Mom, I saw you and Mike sitting out there this morning. Why did he look so sad?"

"Well, I was telling him about the pain Dad and I have been going through with his sickness, and we were talking about how we think Dad only has a year or two to live. Then, I told him about Uncle Louis and everything you've been dealing with… and then Mike told me about his own suffering."

I didn't even have time to complain that she told my brother before I had a chance to, and then I heard her say that Mike was suffering too.

"What is he suffering about, mom? Was it Uncle Louis?"

That jerk. I'm going to lose it!

"No, Gina. It was Jim Everett."

"What?!"

"He told me all these things about how Jim Everett pretended to be his friend and ended up sexually abusing him and threatening him not to tell. Mike was only six or so at the time, and we thought they were best friends. We had no idea."

She continued. "Mike said that Jim Everett's father must have abused him and that that's where he must have learned the horrible things that he did to Mike. Mike said that in class Jim would give him looks across the room. He called him a faggot in front of other kids and threatened him both silently and verbally that he would kill him if he ever told."

I could barely breathe. I was strangled by anger against Jim Everett and deep sadness for my brother. I went downstairs, laid down, and took a Xanax. Doug came to check on me, and I told him what I had just heard. I felt so outside of this world, looking down bewildered at how such atrocities can happen. I didn't know what to feel, say or do. I wanted to rush to my brother and hug him, but he was playing with his son. You can't just bring something like this up during a sunny afternoon at the beach with everyone around.

But what's more important? Why is life like this?

When Mike was in high school, his best friend Ronny had committed suicide one day after school. It was one thing after another for Mike, and the pain that I felt for him in the past sometimes became too much to bear. And now, with this new knowledge, I was overwhelmed.

I always loved my brother, and he always loved me. As a child, he protected me. But, he didn't know. And, I didn't know. All I knew was that we were very different and that we each had our challenges.

Growing up, Mike's shyness and introversion were obvious to everyone. He kept everything to himself. His face would turn red in front of people. Despite a highly superior intellect and mechanical aptitude, he couldn't concentrate and had trouble getting passing grades. He always, always looked nervous, and he rarely smiled. Our only explanation was, "Mike is really shy."

It's always so good to spend time with my brother. And, at the same time, it's always difficult and sad. Mike has had such a hard life, and he has problems coping with everything that has happened to him. I would do anything to help him, and yet it's impossible. I can't take away his wounds.

Our Outer Banks vacation was about to end the next day. Everyone was cleaning up for dinner, and Mike came to see if I wanted to go for a scooter ride.

We met downstairs and headed out. The sun was shining, families were out on their decks, kids were playing in the street. Mike let me ride ahead of him, and he followed behind. We kept going, up Poteskeet, around and through the neighborhoods in Duck.

When is he going to start talking? I know what he wants to talk about.

He pulled over in the shade, and I came over. He was quiet and waited.

"I don't know how to say this," he said.

"Mom already told me," I said, trying to help him get through the story quickly.

"She did? Wait, what are you talking about?"

"About Jim Everett or whatever," I said.

"I wanted to tell you myself," he said, angrily.

"Well, she didn't really tell me details."

We had to move because a family on bikes was coming up behind us. We went to the corner shopping center and parked in front of the bakery.

"I've been living in hell," he said.

"I know. I'm so sorry." I started to cry.

"No, don't be sorry. I want to help you. I know what you're going through, and I want to help you," he said.

"I want to help you," I said. "I feel so awful."

"Maybe we can find a way to help other people together. There has to be a better way than this to live."

"I don't want to live at all."

"Gina!"

"It's true."

"I love you, and I'll help you," he said, and he put his arms around me.

"I love you too. I just don't understand how people are so mean," I said, tears pouring down my cheeks.

"I know. If everyone had been through just one day of what you and I have experienced, the world would be a more sympathetic place."

We were both crying. Right there in front of the busy shopping center, we hugged each other tightly and said that it would be okay.

You have no idea how much I love you. I would do anything to take away your pain. I'm so sorry.

In the waiting room, I silently reassured myself
about how normal I am compared to the other
people there, who probably aren't functioning. I thought
through the key points that I wanted to cover with the doctor,
and decided that I should highlight that I feel like I'm at the
end of my rope, I'm in a crisis over what I just found out about
my brother, and although I've always wanted to avoid being
on a long term daily medication plan, now is the time to re-
consider.

Right on time, Dr. Patel entered the waiting room and
called my name.

*I don't like that. I think it would be better if they used
patient numbers or something. Why does everyone here need
to know my name?*

We both sat down in her office and began covering why I was here. I gave a summary of my history, glossing over the details. Half the time, I felt like I was looking down on myself, watching in disbelief as I calmly and unfeelingly explained what I had been through and what I was experiencing.

"Are you suicidal or homicidal?" she asked.

"I always think about killing myself, but I would never actually do it. I think it's wrong, and I would never do it. I just frequently wish I was dead because my anxiety and the memories and the stress – it's just too much to bear sometimes."

I need to get back to work. I wonder if those guys had a chance to look at the estimates. I should send an email reminder about the proposal. The deadline is Tuesday, but I'd like to get it in sooner to show how interested we are in winning the work. We need to increase our urgency of responding to clients. It should take priority over everything else. What time is it? Did I turn my BlackBerry off? I need to be back by noon for that strategy meeting.

"What about hurting someone else? Are you homicidal?"

"Uhh. Well, my one abuser is dead, so that's not an option," I grinned. "And the other one lives outside of the country, so nothing to worry about there. But, I will say that I'm really angry, and I don't know what I would do if I saw him. So I'm staying away," I said with a big, controlled smile. "You know, I feel like I really understand people who kill their abusers. I'm not saying it's right, but I've felt that feeling, and I don't blame them."

Shut up or she's going to commit you.

"But the short answer is, no, I'm not homicidal. I wouldn't kill anyone."

She smiled back. "That's a good thing."

I giggled in agreement.

"I'm professional at keeping myself under control. I've mastered that," I assured her.

"You put on a happy face, like everything's okay."

"Exactly. That's how I keep going. Externally, I'm high-functioning, social, and productive. But on the inside, I'm tormented. I have always distracted myself by diving into my work, and I'm just recently learning to live a more balanced life."

After an hour of interviewing me, the doctor pulled out some charts. The first one was titled, bi-polar disorder.

Oh God. Oh my gosh, no way. I'm not bi-polar. Don't even say it.

"If you look at the list of symptoms here, you don't have any of these except this one here – feeling empty."

Phew.

"Right."

"So this clearly isn't you."

"Right, I would say definitely not bi-polar."

Why am I being critical of someone who is bi-polar? It's not their fault. Thank God I'm not bi-polar.

"What about this one?" she asked, pointing to the general anxiety brochure.

I scanned the list of symptoms and commented on each one. "Yes, yes, yes, uh – maybe, yes, yes, and definitely yes."

"Yes, so let me explain this." She took out a blank sheet and began drawing a Venn diagram. Three overlapping circles, one captioned depressed, one captioned psychotic, and one captioned PTSD.

Holy crap. Psychotic? Stay calm. I'm not going to be admitted. Don't you dare point to that circle and say that's me. I'm on my way back to work; I'm not psychotic. Psychotic is crazy people. People in jail, people who cut themselves. What about that time in high school when I made that girl punch me so that I could have a black eye? And, the first time she didn't hit me hard enough, so I made her hit me again.

Sometimes I like feeling pain, and I like to show pain. Why is that? You know, it really would be a good break to go into the hospital right now for about a month. I could just relax for once, forget about all of my responsibilities, sleep all day. I'm so burned out. Anyway, that's not an option. I can make it through this. I'm not going to quit. Just give me some medication so I can get back to the office.

"So, spectrum anxiety can be seen as a cross-section of all three of these. It falls somewhere in the middle and usually has characteristics of each of these."

She asked, "Do you feel that you are experiencing anxiety and PTSD?"

"Yes, absolutely."

"Okay then. I would agree. So let's look at a few medications that are approved for treatment of those symptoms."

She didn't highlight psychotic. Okay.

She popped out her PDA and came and sat right next to me. She clicked the stylus on PTSD, and a list of medications loaded.

"Have you tried any of these before?" she asked.

"I've never seen a psychiatrist before, but when these issues first came up for me six years ago, my family doctor prescribed Zoloft. I tried that, and it was horrible, so I stopped after one dose. I became highly enraged and was afraid of what I might do. For no good reason, I was directing my rage at my husband, who is the greatest, sweetest guy. It was as if I was projecting the feelings I had toward the abuse on him, or whatever. I was having violent visions, and I felt shaky, scared, unsure of myself, and generally horrible. I thought I was really going to smash his face in. It was terrifying. I was too scared to tell him, and too scared to move for fear of what I might do. I wasn't about to take that kind of medication again."

"Okay, I'm just taking notes."

"Then last year, I felt like I was at having a breakdown and decided to try something else. So, together with my doctor, we agreed on Effexor XR, since it seemed to be working well for my brother, who has always had anxiety. Again, the first pill was a bad experience. I couldn't sleep, my heart was racing and beating out of my chest, and this time I felt terrified. I don't know what these drugs are, but they seem to have a terrible effect on me."

"Have you tried any other anxiety medications?"

"The only other medication I have ever tried is Xanax, and my doctor said that I should take it as rarely as possible, only for severe anxiety. She prescribed me 30 pills in January, and I ran out yesterday. She said I should take it no more than once or twice a year. You can see that I've been taking about 5 per month. Xanax seems to help; it takes the edge off. But I'm worried about the addiction. This week has been particularly bad because I just got back from a family vacation where I found out my brother was sexually abused by another boy when he was six. It's too much to take. I'm overwhelmed. I would prefer not to take any medication at all, but at this point, I need something badly. Should I just keep asking for Xanax and take it when I need it?"

"Here's the thing," she replied. Xanax is a tranquilizer. When you take it, it's like drinking. It masks the problem. You need to take something that actually addresses the symptoms, like one of these."

She pointed to the list of medications approved for anxiety and PTSD.

"When your doctor prescribed the Zoloft and Effexor to you, she should have directed you to take a Xanax in conjunction with them, until you had gotten used to them. You've been blocking out your feelings, and these medications cause all of your feelings to come back. Xanax can help you to gradually get used to that new way of being."

"Okay, that makes sense."

We looked through the list again. I pointed out that I had heard good things about Lexapro. Together we decided on trying that.

"What if I become enraged when I take it? Or, terrified?"

"You're going to take a Xanax with it, and after a few minutes if you are overwhelmed by those feelings, you'll take one more Xanax and you'll be fine. You'll get used to it."

I left Dr. Patel feeling very encouraged.

Afraid of the unknown side effects, I waited until a Friday night to try Lexapro. The weekend would provide enough time to adjust before having to go back to work.

I sat down with Doug on the couch and said, "Okay, honey, I'm about to try my medicine. Hopefully I'll be okay, but if I turn crazy, get me some help okay?" Doug was glad that I was going to try some drugs. My anxiety had been nearly out of control, and I needed help.

I kept a log of my first Lexapro experience:

5:00pm – took Lexapro and ½ of a Xanax

5:10pm – minor trouble catching my breath, lung tightness

5:12pm – took another ½ of a Xanax

5:15pm – felt better

5:30pm – tired. Did some emails, felt a bit slow (prob Xanax)

6:00pm – went to sleep

9:30pm – woke up, mind racing. Brightness of the room and TV and clock bothering me. Everything looks so bright. Sounds bothering me. Everything is loud.

9:40pm – took a bath

10:00pm – went to sleep

Since starting Lexapro, I noticed brightness, softness, noise and temperature more than before. Over the next three weeks, I either got used to it, or those sensory impacts went away.

I started taking Lexapro every day, and I began to feel like myself – more positive, and less worried.

Toby and I had met through a business networking organization. We were both at similar places in our careers and had many characteristics in common. Both of us reported directly to our executive leadership and were highly valued in our firms. We were extremely driven and focused on career growth, unusually hard-working and results-oriented, and continually intent on achieving more and more at a seemingly ever-increasing speed. We also had an attitude and sense of humor in common. Toby cracks me up.

We worked together on business projects for almost a year, and over time our relationship evolved from networking to coffee to polite friendship. At least, I felt like it was a friendship.

There was something about Toby that made her pull away. Just when we were having a good conversation, she would rush off the phone. Or, toward the end of a fun coffee meeting, she would shut down the discussion. And, although I knew we both enjoyed each other's company, I sometimes felt uncomfortable calling her or asking her to have lunch. I got mixed signals on whether she wanted a friendship.

So, one day I just brought it up.

"This sounds really weird," I started, "because it's not like we've known each other for that long. Anyway, I have a great connection with you and really enjoy our friendship, but sometimes get the vibe that you don't really want to be close friends. It's very hard to explain, but it's as if you only want to hang out and be friends to a certain extent but then that you want to cut it off. It sounds very fifth grade, but I can't tell if you like me or don't like me, or what's really going on."

"Do you really think that?" she replied. "I really like you and hate that it seems like I don't."

"It's just a little uncomfortable. Is there something I'm doing or saying?"

"No. I had no idea."

"It's no big deal, I just thought I'd bring it up."

"Wow. I'm glad you did."

We talked it through, but not too deeply. It was probably one of the longest conversations we had ever had. We rehashed our lunches, meetings, phone calls, and some of the different scenarios. We talked at a high level about her difficulty connecting with people in general – and about people's tendency to think she's a snob.

"We'll have to talk more about this," she said, and that's how we ended it that day.

No big deal. Just good to know.

We continued to talk, somewhat tentatively, about the invisible barrier between Toby and other people and even the distance between Toby and her husband.

A few weeks later, I got a call from Toby, who sounded a little out of sorts. She said that she'd figured out that she chose her husband because he let her keep him at a distance.

"I only let people get so close, and then I shut them out," she said. "The reason I married Matt is because he expects virtually nothing from me emotionally. The cost of being off the hook there is that he demands a lot of physical caretaking."

She went on to say that her inability to have a "real" relationship with anyone was making her life increasingly difficult.

I couldn't believe that she was opening up. Several conversations later, we both told each other a bit more, mentioning childhood problems and abuse at a high level. We both acknowledged that we had issues but didn't go much further than that. Both of us knew, though, that this discussion would continue when we were ready.

In the meantime, Toby took these latest realizations to heart and made some big changes in her life, including switching to a lower pressure job and setting some different boundaries in her marriage.

We laughed about the way we had both become, which helped. "Driven over-achievers" and "smiling suicidals," we called ourselves, joking because we're so strong and happy on the outside and tortured on the inside. It was good to have a friend who had the same coping mechanisms as me. I didn't know the details, but I knew enough to know that we had some of the same damages.

Toby and I were scheduled to have lunch to "talk about things". It was unspoken, but I knew she was about to tell me more. It was no secret that she was having a tough time and I wanted to give her the opening if she wanted my support. Two hours before our lunch, I got this email from Toby:

"Don't read on if you think this will freak you out...
but I wanted to give you a little context on everything, since it
might be hard to fill you in on all of this in the middle of our
lunch . . . . I've just come to a new understanding of my whole
life . . . my addiction to achievement, lack of connection with
others (and myself), the difficulties in my marriage, ongoing
depression, etc.

"I started using achievement as a way to numb myself
as a kid. My childhood was pretty unhappy – my grandfather
sexually abused me starting from the time I was 9 through age
14. When I was 10 I told my mother, who did not help me.
After I told her, she never looked me in the eye or touched me
again. In fact, she did everything in her power to sabotage my
relationships - all in an effort to prevent me from talking about
what was happening. All of my drive came out of that
desperation – the need to deny the reality of what was
happening to me."

"I left home at 17 and when I was 19 spend my junior
year abroad in the UK. It was a pretty exciting time and I
soaked in everything, traveling 3 days most weeks and
covering more than 8 countries. Toward the end of that year I
was gang raped by a fellow student and two of his friends."

"I've dealt with a lot of this, but have always
'pretended' it was fine to the world. The pretending has served

me well – I'm well-liked, well-networked, everyone's friend, but close to no one. The pretending has disconnected me from myself and from other people."

"I've always thought I could disconnect myself from the past and reinvent myself as in a way that made it irrelevant. Not true! For more than two decades I've suffered from crippling depression alternating with elation – the depression routed in the denial, and the elation attached to achieving 'just one more' thing. I've always thought I could escape the past if I did enough well enough."

"I am in the process of accepting my entire story and the impact my history has had on my sense of self, my relationships, choices, role as a mother, wife, daughter, sister, friend. And accepting all of the parts of my story gives me the chance to be a whole person."

We had lunch two hours later. There's just no way to put words to how upsetting life can be, and there's no right way to address everything I just read. But we talked, and we sympathized, and we both understood. We are who we are because of what we've experienced. And we're both learning to accept that and to become better at being who we really are.

An unrecognized number on my cell phone caller ID caught me trying to relax by the pool.

"Hello, this is Gina," I answered.

"Hi Gina, this is Tania from the family counseling center at Prince William. You wanted to schedule an appointment with us?"

Aah, it's the psychotherapy practice that Dr. Patel referred me to.

"Oh, yes, please."

"I have an opening this Wednesday the 11th at 11am. Are you able to come in during the day?"

"Well, during the day works, but unfortunately, not this Wednesday. I'm out of town with my in-laws this week. Do you have anything open the last week in July?"

My mom must have faxed in the new patient form that I was planning on sending in when I got back from vacation. She probably stopped by and saw it sitting there and wanted to help.

"End of July?" she almost barked, "Why do you want to wait so long?!"

"Well, as I mentioned, I'm out of town right now, and then I'll have to clear my calendar when I get back. My schedule is flexible, but I have to work around client meetings and business travel. I'd also like to coordinate with other appointments so that I don't have to take so much time away from work. And, Dr. Patel also just put me on some medication last week, and I'd like to get used to that and see how things are going before I come in for counseling."

"Well, I don't think you should be waiting. If you're suffering from anxiety and PTSD, you need to get in here right away."

Why is she taking this tone with me? Is the goal to make me more anxious?

"Okay, well, I actually went through about six months of intensive psychotherapy already, so I've gotten some help. It's important but I'm not in an emergency."

"Well, you need to get in here right away, and you don't just come to therapy once a month, you know."

"Uh, ok. How often do I need to come?"

"Once a week – at least."

"Ok, well do you have an opening on August 2nd, and I can start that day? I actually have an appointment with Dr. Patel to check my medication, and it would be easier for work if I could do both on the same day, since I'm all the way in Herndon."

"You can't do that. Your insurance isn't going to cover two appointments on the same day."

"Really? The other appointment is with a psychiatrist – it's not therapy. It's just a 15-minute appointment to make sure that my medication is working out."

"It doesn't matter. The doctor may write that she provided you some counseling, and the insurance won't cover another therapy appointment. They're not going to let you have two appointments on the same day."

What a bitch. Is this the lady that would be counseling me?

"Okay, so how long do I need in between appointments, then?" I asked.

"They need to be on two different days. You need to call your insurance company."

"Okay, I'll give them a call and then call you back."

Never. Like I would really want to be counseled by her! Forget the therapy for now. And, when I'm ready, I'll go back to Dr. Young.

Fifteen minutes was all we had scheduled this time, and the goal was to ensure that my medication was working well and that the anxiety was going away. I explained what was going on, and how I generally felt better.

"Some of the side effects are becoming disturbing, though," I said. "The benefits definitely outweigh the problems, but maybe there's something else that would help."

I described how although emotionally I didn't feel anxious, physically I did. I found myself making repetitive movements such as squeezing my hands together, stretching my eyes, kicking my feet.

"I don't know if it's the Xanax wearing off or if it's the Lexapro, but I'm having a lot of trouble physically relaxing now."

"That's a common side effect of benzodiazepines," Dr. Patel explained. "Xanax has a short half-life, and when it wears off, you may experience physical anxiety. Would you be comfortable trying something a little stronger?"

Again, we looked through the list of drugs in her PDA, and together we settled on Clonazepam, which has a 35-hour half life. I started taking that the following weekend, and the jitters and physical irritation disappeared. And, within ½ hour of taking the pill every night, I was asleep. So, for the first time in years, I consistently had a good sleep. I slept like a log.

I was a bit tired, but I was glad to be here, and that's a lot to say for me. I was enjoying my morning so far. It was Sunday – the day when I'm usually the most anxious, worrying about the coming week and thinking of all I need to do to be successful at work. I was should-ing myself over and over about getting started on that statement of work, or at least taking care of some other action items before the weekend was over, to lighten Monday's load. As usual, I couldn't help thinking about everyone's expectations of me and how I could exceed perfection with my clients, my colleagues, and others in the business environment where I typically perform so well.

The Lexapro really seemed to be working. The obsession with dying was pretty much gone. Now, when I drive home, I don't wish someone would just blast into me at

100 miles per hour and knock me into oblivion. When I lay down at night, I don't feel so exhausted and wish that I'll just never wake up. I don't think about how much easier it would be if I didn't have to live another day feeling so bad.

I'm convinced that I've never been suicidal; I just have had an overwhelming desire to not live anymore.

If thinking about dying all the time isn't suicidal, then what is?

I have a wonderful husband and family, a great job, and I'm fortunate to have everything that I have. With the medication, when I make this affirmation, I also feel it, and I feel good. Well, relatively good.

*J*ust say it. He's always supportive. What could you possibly be afraid of now? I'm worried about what he'll think.

"I'm thinking about taking legal action against my uncle," I blurted out to Doug as we lay there watching a rerun of "The Office."

I should have told him about this earlier, but I wasn't sure if I was going to do it. Now I'm sure.

"Really?" he asked. "Why is that?"

"I just feel like I want to. I feel like it's going to give me some sort of justice. I can't stand to let him get away with what he's done. You know how he sent me that letter?"

"Yeah. Where he admitted stuff?"

"Yes. Well, I've emailed him back a couple of times, and I sent him one last weekend asking why he hasn't replied to me. And he didn't reply. Again. I told my mom, and she said that she heard he had hired a lawyer because he's scared of what's going to happen to him. Supposedly he's been advised to not speak to me and to not have anything to do with anyone in the family. He's not supposed to go to family gatherings or have communication with any of us."

"Wow."

"So anyway, he's scared and feeling guilty. I want to lodge some type of formal complaint and seek some justice."

"So, how are you going to do that?"

"I'm not really sure. But, I was thinking of talking to a personal injury lawyer – one who deals with childhood sexual abuse cases. If I could get some type of settlement, it would fund that retreat I'd like to have, or the book, or whatever I decide to do to help other people who are dealing with this crap."

"Huh. And, when are you going to do that?"

"I don't know. Soon."

The next morning I was on the web searching for local law firms with the type of experience I needed. I picked one that was located on the same street as a consulting firm I used to work for and got voicemail. Next on the list was one in Arlington.

"Weimer, Rosenberg & Gold," said a friendly young voice on the other end.

"Hello. My name is Gina McCabe, and I was hoping to talk to an attorney who deals with childhood sexual abuse. Is there someone like that in your office?"

"Yes, there is. Alexandra Rosenberg works with those types of cases, and she would be a great person to talk to. She happens to be on a call right now, so I'd like to have her call you back later today."

"Okay, great. Thanks"

"In the meantime, it would be helpful if I got a bit more information from you. Is now a good time to talk, and are you comfortable sharing some further details with me?"

"Sure, yes."

We started with the contact information, date of birth type of stuff. It was much like making a first-time doctor's appointment, except that Nicole was a lot friendlier and sounded like she really cared.

"Okay, now who is the person who was injured?"

"Uh, that would be me."

"Okay. Now, I'm going to ask you several questions, some of which are pretty personal and may be uncomfortable. If, when we get to those, there are any areas that you don't want to cover for whatever reason, please just let me know,

and we can skip those. I completely understand and don't want
to make you uncomfortable."

I like this girl.

"Okay, no problem."

"Ready?"

"Ready."

By then, I had talked about this abuse mess enough to
be able to rattle the stories off without too much distress.
Actually, I was probably more disconnected to it than
anything.

"Who was the abuser?"

"My uncle."

"What's his name?"

"Louis Lambert."

"Got it."

"And do you have the address?"

"I do, but I can't remember it right now. Can I get
back to you on that? It's in Quebec."

"Sure, that's fine. And, would you happen to have any
photos of him?"

"Uh, not hanging in my house or anything, but I could
definitely get one from my parents without a problem."

"Okay, good."

"And, how old were you when this happened?"

"Um, around two or three. Until probably eight or nine."

"And, where did it occur?"

"Well, it happened at his house, our house, my grandparents' house. Basically, he tried every time I saw him. I was terrified. Whenever he was around, I was afraid, and I needed to act normal yet felt like I wanted to run and hide. He would always try to grab me, kiss me, touch me, rub me, get inside my clothes. He was very aggressive and always made inappropriate comments, too. I recognized very early on that I needed to stay away from him, so I was often able to push him away or wiggle my way out and run off."

"When it happened, how long did it last?"

"What, the abuse?"

"Yes."

"Well, it wasn't the abuse that lasted so long but the terror. I remember my brother and I being sent to stay at their house, for example, and I was terrified the whole night, knowing that my uncle was always trying to molest me."

"And when that happened, was it like minutes or hours?"

"I guess minutes but it felt like hours."

I told Nicole about how long I had lived in denial and how I was unwilling to even admit to myself what had

happened. I told her about the panic attack I had in the tub
right before our wedding.

"Gina, I'm so sorry about all of this. Your wedding is
supposed to be such a happy time, and it's terrible to think that
you were going through so much turmoil."

That had made me feel so good. It amazes me when
someone hears something so uncomfortable and responds with
such an appropriate and heartfelt thought. I was glad to have
selected this firm and was looking forward to speaking with
Alexandra Rosenberg.

Two days later, she called.

"Hello, this is Gina."

"Hi Gina, this is Alexandra Rosenberg of Weimer,
Rosenberg & Gold in Arlington. I'm returning your call from
Thursday."

"Oh, yes. Thanks so much for giving me a call back."

"Listen, I reviewed the information that you provided
our administrative staff, and unfortunately since we're not
licensed in Quebec, we're not going to be able to help you
with this. However, I've reached out to a close friend of mine
in that area who has a lot of legal contacts in Montreal. I'm
also going to search the American Association for Justice
membership and see who I can find in the Montreal area for
you."

"Okay, that would be great."

"I wanted to give you a call back personally to tell you how much I truly believe in what you're doing, and I wish you the very best."

"I appreciate that, Alexandra. Thank you."

All I cared about was getting this major side effect under control. We walked down the hall to her office as if we were old friends going for coffee.

"So, how are you doing?" Dr. Patel asked, with a smile.

"Very well, thanks," I replied, sitting down on the leather couch.

I really am feeling good. Except for the sex thing, though. I want to ask her about that.

We went through all of the regular questions to make sure that I wasn't in danger of killing myself or someone else.

"I have to ask these questions," she re-assured me.

"I know," I grinned. "That's good."

"So how is your anxiety?"

"It's much better than it used to be, but is it possible that I'm already building up a tolerance to the Lexapro? Because twice this week I had what I would call minor-almost panic attacks. Like, I was about to panic but then it was so minor that I was fine.

"You're at a very low dosage of Lexapro. You wouldn't be building up a tolerance, but maybe we should get you up to twenty milligrams per day instead of ten. You can try it, and see how it goes. We can always switch back."

"Okay. And I wanted to ask you about something else also."

This is embarrassing.

"Sure."

"Well, I have no sex drive whatsoever. I'm pretty sure it's the medication, because if I skip it, then my sex drive is normal."

"Yes, this is the worst part about this kind of medication. It affects the libido. There's something else you could take that often helps with that. Have you ever heard of Trazedone?"

"No. And I have to say that I feel like I'm already taking a ridiculous amount of drugs. I would rather not take anything else."

"That's fine. I'll give you a prescription for Trazedone, and you can try it. You can just take it as needed, not necessarily every day."

How does she know I won't need it every day? Ha ha. Well, I should try it. I can't stand this not having sex stuff.

"They say that men are easily aroused," she began.

I giggled as if to say, "no sh*" and smiled.

"But women are so different," she continued.

I know; trust me.

"Sometimes it helps if couples spend a lot of time together. Women need a lot more intimacy."

"Doug and I have a very intimate relationship. He's extremely loving and caring... and patient. We spend a ton of time together, and he does all the right things. It's my brain that won't respond."

"Yes, unfortunately that's a side effect. Try the Trazedone. See how it works."

We wrapped up the appointment, and I went straight to CVS and turned in my refill prescriptions as well as this Trazedone stuff, hoping that I might get lucky with it.

I read all of the directions and precautions as usual, and popped one. Nothing.

She said it was supposed to take effect within half an hour and then that I would get really tired.

But nothing. Doug was already sleeping and soon I fell asleep too.

Around midnight I woke up and couldn't breathe through my nose. I was suddenly all congested.

What, did I suddenly get a cold?

I kept trying to sleep with my mouth open, but every time I fell asleep, I would automatically revert to the nose breathing and couldn't get any air in. All night, I tossed and turned.

I can't believe I'm sick.

Over the next half day, the nasal congestion got better and better. I was so sleepy, though, and ended up taking a two hour nap mid-day. By nighttime, the congestion was completely gone.

It's that Trazedone!

I read the prescription pamphlet again, and there it was under the side effects section: nasal congestion, bad taste in the mouth, dry mouth.

I guess Trazedone isn't going to do it for me. Oh well, I tried it. And on top of the terrible stuffy nose, I didn't feel the least bit sexy.

It was a travel day, this time to New York City, for a client meeting. My flight back wasn't until late, so I spent the evening waiting at the airport and doing some work online.

I should look for an attorney in Montreal.

I repeated the same search that I had previously queried in Virginia, this time looking for child sexual abuse lawyers in Montreal, Quebec. Before I knew it, two hours had passed, and I still had not found a single Montreal firm mentioning child sexual abuse. The firms specializing in personal injury had marketing messages focused on medical malpractice, workplace injury, and every other type of negligence except the one I needed.

I picked a personal injury firm and called.

"Hi, my name is Gina McCabe, and I'm looking for an attorney that can help me with a child sexual abuse case. Would there be someone in your practice who specializes in that area?"

The gentleman on the other end of the line proceeded with a brief interview to get a better idea of my needs. He told me two or three times over that it's extremely difficult to win a child sexual abuse case in Canada. Those who do win typically receive very, very small settlements.

He wrapped up with, "If you would like to proceed, we would need to put together an agreement for representation, and we would require some sort of deposit . . .".

I interrupted. "So, you would work on retainer as opposed to taking a percentage of the settlement?"

"That's correct. In cases like these where our firm is taking on a lot of risk with little likelihood of success, we work on a retainer basis."

"Okay, well thank you very much." I hung up.

How uplifting! Very high risk, very little chance of winning the case, having to pay up front in order to lodge a formal complaint against someone who abused me. Awesome!

I picked another one from the personal injury search results, called and gave the same opening line. This time, what

seemed like a friendlier gentleman on the other end asked me
a few questions and said that he would check and get right
back to me.

Within a half hour, I got a call back. He suggested that
I should email a scan of the letter that my uncle sent me to
Samuel Weinstein & Associates, along with my uncle's name
and address. The firm would look into his social status and
determine which type of case – criminal or civil – would be
the best option.

"If your uncle is on welfare," he explained, "then the
settlement would come from the government and taxpayers;
that can take a long time and be more difficult. If your uncle is
not on welfare, then a civil case would call for settlement from
his own finances; that typically takes less time and is simpler."

"To give you an idea of where I'm coming from," I
said, "I don't really care about the money."

I'm thinking out loud here.

"What I really want is justice. I've been in denial for
so long, living my life in fear and shame, and for the first time
in my life I want to stop being afraid, and I want to confront
him. I want him to pay for what he did, I want to make sure
he's unable to hurt anyone else."

I'm pissed.

"Well, you certainly sound like you've made up your mind in pursuing this. We'll take a look at the materials that you send us and will determine the best path."

"Sounds great, thank you."

My flight landed at Dulles at 7:15pm, and I was home by 9:00. I dropped my bag, hugged and kissed Doug, and went straight to the scanner. I emailed scans of the letter – both pages, the envelope, the postal registration slip, and my email response to him – waiting anxiously for a reply.

The next day, Alexandra Rosenberg called me again to let me know that she had mailed me a couple of names of what she called "big-time" attorneys in the Montreal area who she assured me would either be able to help or direct me to someone else who could. She gave me information about a woman who was a mutual friend of hers as well as these fellow lawyers and suggested that I should mention the relationship.

I've actually already made a few calls, but this will be really helpful in case those don't work out.

As promised, a letter arrived at my home address that afternoon, and along with Alexandra's business card was a list of firms with their contact information and their areas of specialization.

Nice stationery. Old school mail.

She had circled the firms that I should call and made notes in the margins. I noticed that she had highlighted Samuel Weinstein.

Good. That's the firm I spoke with yesterday. I can't believe she's making all this effort to help me. How nice.

I have been fortunate in life to have many really good friends. But it had been years since I had developed a new close friendship.

When I met Lexy, our friendship was immediate. She was funny, beautiful, poised and full of positive energy. The first time we met at a networking event together, I invited her over to dinner, and within half an hour we were talking about deep, real stuff. We laughed about how we went "right there."

We will be friends for life. I just know it.

Lexy texts more than anyone I know, and I love it. She'll send me, "What are the McCabes up to today? I'm watching 'The Hills' and eating Tostitos. Who are these people?" And I'll text back, "I'm doing a facial and eating a burrito right now. Call me after Sunset Tan." We'll go back and forth like this twenty times until real life takes over.

One Friday, after a few months of knowing each other, Lexy texted me, "What are you up to, G?"

I replied, "Writing."

"Writing what?"

"A book."

"About what?"

"Well, it's kind of a story about Gina McCabe, focused on a certain aspect."

I don't want to tell her. She'll think I'm gross.

"Oh, well I'd love to read it. Send me a copy and I'll read it on the beach tomorrow."

"Uh, it's not exactly uplifting."

"Oh no. What's it about?"

"It's just not a rosy story, that's all."

I totally don't want to send it to her. What if she thinks I'm crazy and won't want to be friends anymore?

"I'll send it to you so you can take a look."

Oops, I just said that.

Two hours later I got a text. "I'm reading and reading and can't stop. I'm finding that this story hits very close to home. Did you see that I had these behaviors? I don't want to talk right now, but we should talk at some point."

I texted back, "No. I had no idea, Lexy. I'm so sorry!"

Two days later, we caught up by phone.

"The book!" she said.

"The book."

"It was so real to me."

She told me about how she had been molested by a camp counselor in second grade.

"It was all very playful and manipulative, and he tried to play it off like it was nothing," she said, "but every opportunity he had, he would try something."

"I'm so sorry."

"And I remember when I came home, my mom asking me if he hurt me. Of course I denied it, but I don't even know why she asked me that."

What is it with the moms?

"Have you ever gone face to face with her on it?" I asked.

"No. My mom and I are opposites. I'm very open and confrontational, and she avoids confrontation at all costs."

We talked about how in those days parents weren't educated about sexual abuse. Everyone was in denial about it, and no one wanted to talk or hear about it. Things are different today, we agreed. Everyone should know better by now, and it's time to do something.

"You need to publish that book," she said. "There are so many women who are dealing with this."

I couldn't believe how sharing this story resulted in learning of so many other survivors.

The seventies. There wasn't less ugliness back then, just more secrets.

I remember my parents telling me about a rape that had happened in Baie d'Urfe. The victim was a girl who was in my gymnastics class. It was the pretty girl with freckles and shiny red hair. No one really talked about it, but it was just something people in town knew.

A week or so after finding out, I went to gymnastics and she was there. When I saw her in the locker room, I felt confused. I felt like she was bad. I felt that I shouldn't talk to her. Now, as an adult, I would go talk to her and tell her how sorry I was. I would give her a hug and ask if there was anything I could do. I would be her friend and help her to feel safe. I would offer my love and compassion. But, at the time, I didn't want to have anything to do with her. And now I know why.

In those days, I was ashamed and scared. How could I possibly tell anyone what was happening to me? How could I risk the rejection of my family? Why would I want to admit something that was so yucky? I felt bad. And, in my mind, because she was raped, she was like me.

So I pretended like nothing was happening. I denied reality, pushed it so deeply down inside of me that no one would ever have suspected anything. I denied what was my true story because I hated it. I hated myself, and I was only nine years old. I wish I could find that girl and apologize to her, be her friend, and help her.

Tuesday morning, I received an email from the Montreal law firm to which I had reached out a few days ago:

"Dear Gina McCabe,

We are presently studying your file and we have a few questions regarding this matter:

Are we to understand that the letter sent to you by Louis Lambert was both unsigned and undated?

If this is the case, can you fathom any realistic way of getting a properly signed letter from him, or of proving by other means that this letter comes from him?

When was the last instance of abuse? When did the long term negative repercussions of this abuse begin to be felt in your marriage, when did you begin seeing a therapist, and when did you reach the conclusion that the abuse was the source of the problem? These questions are important because we are searching for a means of overcoming some strict prescription periods in civil liability.

Thank you."

I replied:

He did not sign the letter by hand, only typed his name, and there was no date on the actual letter. However, if you look at the postal service registration slip he filled out, it is in his writing, with his name and date. He wanted to make sure the letter got to me, so he registered it. I'm sure that with the original envelope and registration slip, which I have, we could prove that this letter came from him. We could also prove that the letter was sent right after our family reunion, where my family confronted him. I think he would admit writing that letter. I also think that his wife would testify that he wrote the letter.

The last instance of abuse was when I was around age 8, in 1978.

The long term negative repercussions were not felt in my marriage until last year, and that's when I began seeing a therapist, in the spring of 2006. That was the first time that I had admitted the abuse, and that's when I realized that the abuse was the source of the problem. Although I had admitted the abuse to myself and my therapist, I was too afraid and embarrassed to admit what had happened to my husband, my friends, my parents or anyone else. I was too afraid to confront my uncle. In working with the therapist, I was finally able to tell my husband after a month or two, and that's when I really started working through the treatment and getting help. Eventually, I was able to tell my parents, and finally I got up the courage to confront my uncle.

I hope this helps.

Thanks.

Wednesday night I received another email from the Montreal law firm:

"Dear Gina McCabe,

We have examined your case and thank you for your confidence in us. Given the nature of acts alleged and the amount of time that has passed, this could become quite complicated and may have cross-over implications in criminal law. To commit our firm to your case, we will need a retainer of twenty-thousand dollars ($20,000). Furthermore, there is no guarantee that we will win, and even if we do win, there is no guarantee that the defendant is solvent or will be able to pay. You may win a moral victory but not be indemnified financially.

To prove your case, it would be very helpful if your uncle would sign his letter or some other form of confession.

Without that, our procedures may require you, your mother and other people to testify in court here in Quebec.

Please consider all of this very carefully as you are on the verge of embarking upon a difficult battle. We will await your instructions.

Yours very truly."

Wow. Talk about a disappointment! So I need to put twenty K down and continue paying fees, and they have little to no confidence that I will even win a moral victory. Do I take the risk? What value is this effort really going to bring me? I don't want his money. I want an apology. I want to know why he did it. I want to stop him and everyone else like him from the damage they do.

*W*hat did we ever do before the internet!. Look at all the listings for Lambert. Yup, there's his number. That's it! What if he's not home? He's probably going to panic and hang up on me because his lawyers told him not to talk to me or anyone in the family. I need to turn off my caller ID. What if Tante Marianne answers? I deserve to have a conversation with him. After all he's done, he owes me a conversation. I'm not going to do anything. I just want to talk. What am I going to say?

I'm just trying to heal. And I want to know why he did what he did. Was he abused? Why did he do it? Does he know how it made me feel? Is he getting help? I can think about this all day. If I don't go ahead and call him, I'll never know. Who cares what I say. I'm going to try.

I called. It rang twice. I heard it pickup. I could hear my aunt talking in the background. No one spoke on the phone. I said "hello." I heard a hand cover the phone and a man's voice say something muffled in French. He hung up.

I can't believe this. I'm calling back.

I called again. His voice came on, sounding feeble "allo?"

"Hi, it's Gina," I said.

"Allo."

"What's going on?" I asked. "Why did you hang up on me?"

"Uh, we had some trouble with the phone. Half an hour before that it happened to Auntie Marianne. I did not hang up on purpose."

I believed that they had been having problems with the phone, but I didn't believe that this time was an accident. Either way, though, it didn't matter.

"As you know, I've been having a really hard time with things, and I wanted to talk to you about it."

"I would like to have Auntie Marianne listen in on the other line. Is that okay with you?"

"No, it's not okay," I declared. "I just want to talk to you, and I don't want anyone else on the phone. Why do you want her to listen in anyway?"

"Just so that she hears what we're talking about. I've been seeking counsel, also, so I don't know if I'm even supposed to talk to you."

"Well, I need you to talk to me."

"My lawyer says I shouldn't talk to anyone or I could be in trouble."

"Well, I'm not going to do anything. I just want to talk."

Silence.

"So why did you get a lawyer, anyway?" I asked.

"Because I knew that you could do anything to me."

"Like what?"

"I don't know, send the police after me, send someone to hurt me or even kill me."

"I was angry, I'll admit. But I'm not about to hurt anyone. I'm not that kind of person. Can you help me to understand why you did the things you did to me when I was a kid?"

"Well, first of all, the things you accused me of in your letter, like being in a child sex ring, are not true."

"I never accused you of being in a child sex ring. I asked to know what other kids you may have molested so that I could reach out to them and help them with their healing as well."

"Also, you mentioned that I did things right in front of other people, and I never – "

"Not that you did them right in front of other people. That you did them secretly, when other people were there. Not out in the open."

"Gina, I'm very sorry for anything I have done to hurt you." He began to cry. "If you would forgive me, I would really accept that. I don't know if you heard, but I've had two operations this year and I'm getting ready to have another one because I have cancer. I guess I'm really paying for – I don't believe that people pay for what they've done wrong, because that's in God's hands. But I've been suffering probably just as much as you ever since your letter. 2007 has been a really bad year, and several times I've just thought that I need to get out of this because I can't take it."

This is unbelievable. In the same breath, he's asking for forgiveness and telling me how hard he has it. Of course he feels terrible, because he's been caught and confronted. I feel absolutely no sympathy for his illness.

He continued, "You know, you go so far back. I don't even know how you can remember these things. It's like you're saying I was doing things to you before you were born."

Stay calm. Don't freak out or you won't get anything out of him.

"It was so long ago, and you know I've seen you several times since then, and you never said anything to me about it."

"I know it was so long ago. You know why I never said anything about it?" I started to cry and could barely get the words out. "Because I was so upset, confused and disturbed about it that I couldn't even admit what had happened, and I was in complete denial."

"I'm sorry," he said again, still crying. "I wish there was something I could do to fix it. Can you forgive me?"

"I'm working on it. I don't feel ready yet, but I'm working on it. What about Anne-Marie, Luc, Nadia?"

"Nope."

"You never abused them?"

"I'm not a child abuser, Gina."

"Okay, so if you do something sexual to a child that they don't want you to do, that's not abuse?"

"No. I don't believe I'm an abuser."

"Okay, so did you ever have sexual contact or kiss any of my cousins that I mentioned?"

"I have not had sexual contact, ever."

"Okay, how about touching them in their private places?"

"I never intended to touch anyone. You know, when we had family get-togethers, the kids always came over to me. I always had five or six of them on my lap."

"I know. That's because they all loved you because you were a lot of fun."

So, you're saying it's the kids' fault that you abused them?

"So I never intentionally touched anyone, but if they were climbing all over me and I brushed by them by accident, how could I control that?"

Stay calm. As pathetic as this is, it's good. He's admitting it.

"Okay. Have any of them ever confronted you about anything? What about Nadia?"

"Nadia has never said a word. I may have kissed her, but she has never said anything. In fact, she was working on a project on the internet a few years ago, and we communicated by email. I helped her with that. You know, at Grandpapa's funeral, everyone was consoling everyone, and I could have had plenty of opportunities to kiss or touch anyone there, and I didn't."

Does he have any clue how stupid that was to say?

"And what about Luc? Did you ever do anything to him?"

"There has been some accusation that we're not too sure about."

That we're not too sure about. Oh, give me a break!

"What did he accuse you of?"

"He said we were talking about sex, and I attacked him. That's what he claimed."

"Uh huh. So what was it that happened?"

I know exactly what happened. Luc told me this story when I saw him in 1989. You nasty pig.

I'm really good at being calm. I sound very calm right now. This is good.

"He asked me a question about sex. I answered it. Then he says I attacked him."

Why would you be talking to your nephew about sex? And I know it wasn't just talking, by the way. He told me the whole story about how you insisted on showing him how to lubricate himself and masturbate. And, by attack, you mean that you grabbed his privates and went at it. I can see that you've convinced yourself that only a small part of this is true – the part that you can accept. And, you're denying the rest. You're pathetic.

"Well, I know that Luc has had a lot of issues in his life, and he's not doing so well. You don't think his troubles have anything to do with what you did to him?" I asked.

"No. The drugs are there, eh? He chooses the drugs."

"So, tell me, what do you think it is that makes a person like you interested in treating children sexually like they are an adult? Were you abused as a child?" I asked.

"No, never anything like that," he claimed

"Then, what is it that made you do these things?"

"I have no idea," he cried. "I don't know. I can't change the past. I wish there was something I could do to remove it, but I can't."

"For me, it's not so much what happened anymore," I said. "I've been dealing with that. But it's the ways that I've coped with it that I'm having so much trouble with today. You know, being terrified, having panic attacks, being uncomfortable in social situations, having to go to therapy and take medication."

"I'm very sorry for that. I've been suffering on my side too. I'm been very nervous for a year now, ever since your letter."

Right, ever since you were busted.

He asked, "Do you think you'll ever forgive me?"

"I don't know. I'm working on it. I'm not ready yet, but I'm trying."

"What can I do to help you?" he asked.

"I'm just trying to understand right now why you did the things you did."

"All I can say is I'm very sorry."

"Well, it's helpful to talk," I said.

Even if you're lying to me, I know that you know what you did, and I know that you're terrified of what I might do, and I know that you're trying to manage your reputation to save your marriage.

"I'm 63 years old now, and I have this to deal with," he said.

"And I'll have another 40 or 50 years to deal with what you did to me," I replied.

"If you can forgive me, please let me know. You can email me. And, we don't have that thing that shows who called –"

"Caller id."

"Yes. So I did not hang up on you. The phone hung itself up. I'm very glad you called back, otherwise I never would have had the chance to talk to you."

Bull. But whatever.

"Okay," I said.

"I'm very ill and my mouth is very cold. I need to go to get a drink. But Auntie Marianne wants to get on the phone."

"Okay that's fine."

I heard the rustle of the phone being handed over.

She probably wants to apologize. She owes me an apology. She's basically his supporter. Why hasn't she divorced him? Because he would take half her money, according to Quebec law, I've been told.

"Hi Gina," she said.

"Hi."

I'm really annoyed that I have to talk to her right now.

"You know, I'm not telling you this because you're my niece, or because Uncle Louis is my husband, but because I have been starting to become a counselor, and the only way – the only way that you will begin to heal – is through forgiveness."

"Uh huh."

"You have to turn to God, and forge[t] – forgive"

She started to say forget. I don't need this lecture.

She continued, "Only God can heal you, and he can heal you. He can help you to forgive and move on."

"You know, it's not as much about forgiving for me right now. I'm working more on the coping mechanisms that

I've developed to deal with all of this, and I'm just having a hard time functioning with a lot of depression and anxiety, fear, panic, social disorders – that type of thing."

"But forgiveness is the only way. I wish I was further along with my counselor training so I would know more, but I know that that's the beginning."

I heard every word, but I was completely shut down.

"I know you don't want to hear this," she continued, "but I wish you would get a Christian counselor. We have this woman in our church who has helped girls who have been raped, and they've been healed. I don't know if you have someone in your church, but if this woman was near you, or spoke English to start with, I know she could help you."

Uneducated. What a stupid discussion she is trying to have.

"I do have a Christian counselor," I lied.

Actually my therapist is Jewish by birth but is not formally religious. She is spiritual and is a really good person. I want you to get off my back. How can I end this conversation?

"Does he help you by showing you scriptures?

"It's a she. Yes, she does. And I've read the bible all the way through many times."

"But I mean, does she show you specific passages to support your healing, like Isaiah 43?"

"Do not fear, for I am the Lord your God?"

"Yes."

"Yes, I know all about it. Anyway, I didn't call to talk about me. I called because I wanted to understand more about why Uncle Louis did the things he did."

"Well, I hope you can forgive him. I have been praying for you every day that you will be able to forgive and heal. And the only way for you to heal will be if you go back to the cross and realize how much God loves us, the sacrifice of Jesus on the cross for us. You have to rely on his promises."

Okay, so you're basically saying that if I was trusting God, I would be healed by now. So, let's apply that same logic to when I was three years old. If I had been trusting God, I would have been protected from your predator husband? If we trust God, then our lives are healed and perfect? That's about all I can take of this conversation.

"I'm working on all of that. Okay, bye."

"Bye."

I hung up and didn't even wait to listen for an I love you from her, which I felt might have been on its way.

That was f*d up. Of course everyone needs to forgive others for their wrong-doings, and we need to forgive

ourselves. I'm not just going to say "I forgive you" and not
mean it.

So, if I had a niece and she called me up and God
forbid my wonderful husband had done something to her,
would I be lecturing her on the best path to forgive my
husband? NO! First of all, I'd be long gone by now, and I
would be apologizing furiously for whatever he had done, and
I would be helping her to feel better. How about listening?
How about letting me say what I feel instead of you telling me
what you think is best. You don't know what's best for me!

This reminds me of the many lectures from my French
aunts who knew so much better than me about everything in
my life. And all I could think was that they really didn't know
me at all, and they didn't even know themselves.

Ten minutes later I found myself pulling out a Bible to
see if I had gotten the verse right. And, I did! Well, close
enough anyway.

I was half smiling. I was pissed at the boldness of my
aunt and at her ridiculous sermon, even knowing that her
intentions were good. She loves me the best way she knows
how. But I was happy that I talked to my uncle, that he
admitted what he did at some level. I was proud of myself for
having the guts to call him on it! Today was a very good day.

Two months ago I had booked the appointment, after thinking about scheduling it for over ten years.

"I don't care how big the scar is," I told the surgeon. "I want this tattoo gone."

"Alrightey," he agreed.

With every painful stick, I knew I was closer to having it removed.

Once I was numb, he began cutting. All I felt was a tug here and there. Within five minutes I smelled the burn of the cauterizing he had warned me about.

Jab.

"Ouch!" I flinched at the painful sting.

His assistant gave me another stick.

"Do you want us to preserve the tattoo for you in a bottle?" she joked.

"Uh, no thanks. I'm pretty sure I'll be okay without it." I grinned.

As he stitched, he said, "You're going to be fine with this scar. You can tell people it's from gall bladder surgery or something."

"I did have my gall bladder removed, actually, so it'll fit right in with my other scars," I smiled. "But I'm not worried about what anyone thinks, anyway. I'm just glad it's gone."

I wish everything could go away with surgery. Can you remove my sexual abuse for me too?

They bandaged me up and sent me on my way, and four hundred bucks later, I was freed of that one mistake and left with just a scar. I felt good.

The brakes on my convertible A4 quattro squeaked as I turned past Silbersiepen Farm toward my home. I was already three weeks late on scheduling service with Audi. Work has just been too busy, and I'm not willing to cut into my personal time to take my car in. I sipped on my ridiculously customized venti decaf sugar free vanilla skim latte and considered how lucky I am to have access to so many comforts and luxuries.

Paula Cole sang along with Chris Botti's trumpet through my iPod. "What'll I do when you are far away, and I'm so blue, what'll I do?" There was a perfect breeze along the winding roads, and I thought about how much I am loved and supported.

My mom and dad always worked so hard. They gave of their time, energy and money so that we could afford to live in nice neighborhoods and beautiful homes, have good clothes, play sports and take music lessons. They dedicated their lives to our family and taught us to make a positive impact on the world around us. Whatever we wanted, they would find a way to provide.

Had my parents known what was going on, they would have protected me. And the fact that they didn't know is not their fault. I was too ashamed and afraid to tell. I can be angry that they didn't know and still love them unconditionally at the same time. They have always supported and loved me, and had I let them know, they would have helped me all the more. I was too afraid then, but not anymore. Now they know.

Despite my brother and I both keeping our own tragedies from each other for thirty years, we always had a very strong bond and deep love for each other. Healing together and seeking to help others is bringing us even closer.

My husband has been a good listener, fully engaged and asking questions. And from him, that's all I need in order to feel safe and understood. I have connected with him more deeply than anyone in my life now. I have no secrets with him, and I trust him with my deepest darkest troubles. With each day, he further defines and lives out the role of a real husband.

I have friends from every decade, and I keep in touch with almost all of them. Not a single one knows these stories, and I'm sure they'll be surprised. But I'm not afraid, because real friendships are based on truth and openness.

S ix months after my dad's Shy-Drager diagnosis, I finally began to admit to myself how sick he was. Instead of just stopping by or calling whenever I felt like it, I made it a point to put official visits on my calendar so that I could see him more often and for longer blocks of time. Mike had been driving down from Jersey every two weeks to spend time with him, and I went over there at least one day during each weekend. We talked about things that interested Dad like the new iPhone, software programs he was writing as a hobby, goings on in their neighborhood, and things happening at my firm, Doug's fire department job, and Mike's life.

Mike had been having some challenges at home, and I talked about it with my parents, working through ways that we could help him.

"Mike is sometimes very difficult," my dad commented one Saturday.

"Dad, that is so unfair!" I said angrily. "After everything Mike has been through, he's coping the best that he can." I felt the anger coming.

How can someone be so insensitive?

"Mike had a really hard childhood," I said. "Look at all he's been through!"

"When you say a hard childhood, you mean with his depression?" my dad asked.

I looked over at my mom. "Mom, you didn't tell Dad?"

"No," she said, knowing I had wanted her to so that Dad would understand Mike better and be more patient with him.

Dammit, Mom, I told you to tell him way back when we found out. No more secrets!

"Dad," I interrupted angrily, "the reason why Mike is so sensitive, depressed, anxious and has trouble making good choices is because he was raped by Jim Everett when he was six years old. So we all thought Jim was his best friend, yet he was torturing him when Mike went over there. And, he threatened that if Mike ever told anyone, his dad would kill him. So, you wonder why Mike had so many problems in school? How would you feel if you had a guy in your class who had raped you, sitting right behind you, calling you a faggot and threatening to kill you if you told? Mike was terrified. And since no one knew, we always sent him over to Jim's house! And, when Jim's family moved, Mike was sent there for a week at a time to visit. He's been introverted and afraid ever since, constantly worried about fighting off Jim and worried that people would find out."

That was harsh. Maybe I shouldn't have just said that so bluntly.

"Wait a minute," my dad said with a frown, "That doesn't make any sense. Jim Everett was the same age as Mike."

"So what, Dad!" I said. "Supposedly Jim's father sexually abused him, and Jim did the same things to Mike. Mike said that it was torture. It was terrible." I began to bawl. "And look at all of the abusive relationships Mike has been in ever since. The girls he went out with, the friends and co-workers who treated him like crap? He's been abused all his life."

"Well, Mike is still very hard to deal with," he said.

Oh my God. He did not just say that. Does he have no sympathy whatsoever? This, my father, the nicest man I've ever known – all he has to say is sort of "oh well?"

For the first time ever in my life, I just stormed out of their house without another word, letting the door slam, and I drove home. Still crying an hour later, I emailed both of them and wrote that I could not believe the reaction that I had just heard. I explained that Mike needed our support and that he deserved extra special care for his suffering. I called out the many painful experiences that Mike had been through and explained how important it was that we demonstrated our patience and love. Mike just got enough courage to tell us about it this year, and it was a huge step. We needed to show our understanding and help him heal.

My dad didn't respond, but over the next few days, my mom and I exchanged several emails and talked in person. She explained to me that she was unable to tell my dad Mike's story because dad was already facing his own death and the associated emotions that seemed to be almost unbearable for him. She apologized for his response and begged me to forgive him for his inability to process what I had told him. "I talked to Dad about it," she said, "and he says it's just too much for him right now."

I called my dad later, and we talked for a few minutes. At the end of our conversation, I said, "I love you," and his response was "okay." I couldn't believe he wasn't telling me he loved me.

He always tells me he loves me!

Over the next few days, he finally called me back to apologize.

"I do love you, Gina," he said. "We can agree to disagree, right?"

No we can't disagree on this. Mike deserves our understanding, patience and help.

"Yes, we can disagree, Dad," I said, and we left it at that.

Good. It will be easier for me when he dies now ... now that I know he's not so perfect after all.

Crying, I explained to Doug what had happened.

"Your dad can't help it," he said. "It's a lot to take in right now. He's getting sicker and sicker and has his own death to deal with."

"I know," I said, "but it's so sad that he doesn't recognize how much Mike needs from us."

This is the whole problem. We have to be able to tell. We have to be able to listen. We have to be able to accept. And we have to be able to heal together. We can't deny the truth.

During October, my dad's illness progressed from having low blood pressure, fatigue and sensitive bowels to fainting, vision disturbances, and an inability to digest any solid foods. On November 13, he went for a check-up with his gastroenterologist who found a combination of elevated white blood cells, low red blood cells, and a mass on my dad's side. With this news, our disagreement no longer mattered. Doug and I spent every evening following that at the hospital, sitting with my mom while the doctors ran my dad through tests, awaiting confirmation of cancer. Within a day, Mike had called in to work and came down to be with us as well.

We did everything we could to make dad comfortable. We got him his own super soft blankets and pillows and a personal DVD player with three whole seasons of "Everybody Loves Raymond," his favorite show.

The surgeons removed a large section of the bowel and assured us that the self-contained tumor had not spread. Every doctor that stopped by provided further confidence that full recovery was expected.

Ten days after surgery, dad was still struggling, but they agreed to release him in time for Thanksgiving. Having only eaten liquids for five weeks by then, my Dad was thrilled with the ham, stuffing, green beans, mashed potatoes and gravy that my colleagues from the office had sent over. We enjoyed a quiet day, expressing thanks that we were able to once again be together.

Over the next few days, my dad developed severe stomach pain, a fever, nausea and dizziness. We took him back to the hospital, and he was admitted to intensive care with an infection and fluid retention. He was suffering with abdominal pain, difficulty breathing, and, somehow, again, a blocked bowel. The doctors were determined that this was a manageable problem, suggesting a temporary infection and abscess caused by irritation from the surgery, but we had our own opinions about the depth of the problem. He looked more and more ill, frail, and weak every day.

"I want to, once and for all, say that I'm not having any more procedures," he proclaimed. "I'd like them to make me comfortable and send me home."

For nearly two more weeks, they tried everything from blood thinners and antibiotics to fluid aspiration and blood transfusions, but the infection didn't budge, and the colon blockage remained. Finally, the second week in December, we were able to take him home under the care of Hospice of Rapidan.

His first day home was a wonderful day – a bittersweet acknowledgement that he was facing the end of his life surrounded by those who loved him. Doug, Mike and I had setup the living room to accommodate his hospital bed, with linens to match mom's home décor, bouquets of tulips, poinsettias, and some of dad's favorite things. We chatted with him all day, administering morphine and ativan whenever he needed them, adjusting his position and blankets, massaging his feet and hands, and expressing our thanks that he was able to be home.

The next day, my mom's sister Gabrielle and her husband Derek arrived. Dad and Derek had spent so much time together both in younger years and recently, building things together and enjoying each other's company. Dad was so thrilled to have Derek there.

Dad's pain progressed, and along with that came confusion and a diminished ability to express his thoughts. He began to use complex terms that didn't go together, and he related everything back to technology.

Hospice had brought over an automatic drug pump to ensure his comfort since he was unable to communicate his level of pain.

"How's the new pump working, Dad?" I asked.

"It's working great now that I started operating it from the command line," he said.

"You're using the command line on the drug pump?" I asked?

"Yes. It's perfect," he said.

"That's great," I said, learning that it was probably time for me to just agree.

In the afternoon, he began to get agitated. The naso-gastric tube, which he referred to as his network cable, was irritating him, so he ripped it out.

"Now Gina," he said that evening, "when the screen pops up, I want you to click the 'OK' button."

"There's no screen, Dad," I said carefully, ensuring him that I loved him and didn't think he was crazy.

"Yes there is," he slurred. "We just have to find it. We have to click 'OK' to say that we all agree."

"All agree to what?" I asked. My mom and Mike came closer.

"All agree that it's okay for me to leave this place."

"We do agree, Dad," I said, the tears starting. "We know that you're suffering, and you can let go whenever you're ready. We're going to miss you, but we know you have to go, and we're all okay with that. You've been through so much pain, and we all want it to be over."

"Okay. We have to say the commands now," he said, and I want everyone to participate. Derek and Gabrielle too.

"Dad, Derek and Gabrielle are already sleeping," I said.

"What commands do we have to say anyway?" my mom asked. "I don't think we need to say any."

"Yes we do," he said. "Each one of us has to say 'OK' and then it will be okay. First Gina, then me, then mom, then Mike, and so on."

We stood there like the Ya-Ya Sisterhood or a group of kids ready to become blood brothers.

He repeated, "We have to say the commands. Go ahead."

Knowing that saying "Okay" wasn't going to end his life seemed logical, but we were still taking this pretty seriously.

I started.

"Okay," I said, slowly.

"Okay," my dad said.

"Okay," said my mom.

"Okay," Mike said.

There was an uncomfortable pause. As expected, nothing happened. We just held his hands and gently rubbed his forehead.

My dad started again.

"Okay," he said.

Not wanting to hurt his feelings, we continued.

"Okay," I said.

My mom and brother said it too.

By the third time around, we all had tears pouring down our face, and, at the same time, my mom and I were trying not to laugh. Doug was sitting over on the couch, and I looked at him as if to beg him not to think we were as insane as we were acting. He rolled his eyes as if to suggest that we were letting a heavily medicated person worry us over a hallucinogenic ritual.

"Dad, it's fine now. We don't need to say the commands anymore," I said.

"We don't?" he asked.

"No."

"Oh, okay," he said.

"Whenever you're ready, Dad, we're okay with it," Mike said.

"Okay, that's good," he said, and closed his eyes.

He suddenly sat partially up and grabbed his head as if he had a migraine. He winced strongly and stayed there.

We rushed to his side.

"What's wrong, sweetie?" mom asked.

"I need you all to leave the room now."

"Why, Dad?" I asked, beginning to cry.

I'm so confused. Is he going to die right now, or is it just the drugs talking?

"Just go," he exclaimed, with a serious and committed look in his eyes.

We each quickly kissed him on the forehead and left the living room.

Mom and Mike went into the office, and I rushed around the room, turning off the Christmas candles and dimming the lights. I hid in a dark corner where he couldn't see me and cried. I watched him.

Is he going to die right now? God, please give him peace.

He didn't move. He just stared up at the ceiling. I watched his chest, and it was still moving up and down.

He's okay. He's not dying yet.

He stayed perfectly still.

I went in and checked on my mom and Mike, and they were talking about how he was starting to withdraw. We all agreed that, as difficult as it was to say goodbye, we wanted his suffering to stop, and he was ready to die.

"It's been almost an hour. Do you think we can go back in now?" I asked my mom.

"Let me ask him," she said.

We slowly walked over to him and asked if we could come in.

"Oh, sure," he said, as if he had never asked us to leave.

"Are you doing okay?" I asked.

"Yes," he replied, slurring. "I just had to make sure. I had to check and it wasn't my fault and that even being sure I wasn't responsible for what happened here in this judgment time."

In an attempt to translate, my mom said, "And you realized that nothing was your fault and that you weren't responsible for anything bad, right?"

"That's right," he said slowly.

"Dad, you've lived such a great life," I said. "You've been such a good person, a perfect father. I've learned so much from you about being kind, giving and thoughtful. You haven't done anything wrong, and you have nothing to feel bad about. Nothing bad has been your fault. You're the best dad in the world. I love you so much."

"Okay," he said. "I love you too, Gina."

Mike and my mom delivered similar sentiments, and we all cried together for what seemed like the fiftieth time since his initial diagnosis.

My mom had sat by his side every night in the hospital and was now staying on the couch beside him ever since he came home. That night, we all slept in the living room with him.

The next morning, Dad seemed refreshed. He knew that his brother, Paul, from Seattle, was expected in the afternoon, and he seemed to anticipate the visit.

I saw the car pull into the driveway, and I went over to my dad and whispered in his ear.

"Dad, Uncle Paul is here."

"Is he really?" he asked. "No!"

"Yes, he and aunt Paula just pulled in the driveway."

"Oh, Gina," he said, "you always have such good news."

That's funny.

Two minutes later, my dad's brother and his wife walked in the house. I pulled my mom aside.

"Did you warn them about how bad he looks?" I asked her.

"No, but they'll be okay."

"You might want to give them a heads up," I said. "We've been with him every day and have watched the progression, but it might be shocking for them."

"Okay," she said.

They walked in. My dad looked over at his brother and reached his arms out the best he could to welcome him.

He had been unable to smile or make any significant facial expression for weeks, but his eyes were wide and full of welcome for his brother.

For the rest of the day, dad talked more than he had since Derek and Gabrielle's arrival. He couldn't respond appropriately to conversations regarding the short term, but when Paul brought up childhood stories, my dad didn't miss a beat. They recalled their antics on the farm, by the river, and in school. Paul laughed, and my dad said things like, "that was sure funny."

That evening, after waking from a nap, my dad sat half way up and announced that it was time for all of us to go.

"Would everyone please offer to leave the room for my advancement?" he asked. "Either way, the outcome will be consistent," he added, slurring.

"We want to be with you until you go, unless you don't want us here," I said.

"You must assist in disconnecting me from the network, Gina," he said, with frustration at his inability to make sense. "You must continue on my path and reach the ultimate configuration and parameters. And let your great grandfather know that things are okay."

"Dad, I'm not sure what you're talking about, but you have nothing to worry about. You're using such complicated words, and it's hard for me to understand."

"That's just my way of saying that I want you and Doug to go home so that you can go to sleep and so that I can go to sleep. And you can come back and pick me up when you're ready," he said. "And, I meant my great grandfather, not yours."

"Okay," I wept. I hugged him tight and rubbed his shoulders. "Did you see your great grandfather?" I asked.

"Yes."

"What did he say to you?"

"I don't remember."

"Maybe he's just letting you know that it's okay and that you have people who love you and are waiting for you."

"Maybe," he said.

"You've been the best dad in the world," I said. "I have so many wonderful memories of you. You've sacrificed everything for our family, and you've been a shining example of a loving person. I'm so sorry for anything I've ever done or said to put a strain on our relationship. I'm going to miss you, Dad. I love you so much." Tears were pouring down my cheeks and onto his.

"Oh Gina," he said, "Thank you. I love you so much."
He was quivering as he tried to hug me.

I could hear how hard it was for him to talk. Weeks without food and only ice chips to drink, his gums and lips stuck together when he tried to form words.

"Go home now," he said.

"Okay Dad," I said. "I love you."

Doug and Mike came in to each say their goodbyes, and we talked to my mom about how it seemed like he really wanted us to stay away until he passed.

"It seems like it's too hard for him to let go with us here," Mike said.

"That might be the case; I don't know," my mom said.

"Call us if you need anything at all, okay?" I asked her. "And please let us know if something happens, even if it's in the middle of the night. We're going to stay away unless he asks for us."

"Okay, I'll let you know. Thank you."

Mike, Doug and I headed back to my house.

The next day was Sunday, and I went to Bloomingdales to get an outfit for the funeral which I knew wouldn't be far off. Mike stayed at my house and worked on a photo tribute to my dad.

On my way home, I broke down.

I want to go see him. Should I go over there? I wonder
if he would be happy if I stopped by? Or, would it make it
more difficult for him? I always stop by. What if I never see
him again alive? Should I call and ask my mom? I guess I
should just leave him alone so that he can retreat without
pressure. I already miss him. What will I do now? Every time I
go to Best Buy and want to get him a new gadget. A hazelnut
coffee from Starbucks. A smoothie from Panera. Cold Stone
ice cream. Post-it notes. Sweatshirts. I'm always thinking of
him. I love him. Aside from being my father, he's such a good
friend to me.

I wept and continued home.

My alarm was set for 6:00 a.m. Monday to wake me
up for work, but mom called me at 5:30. Doug was just about
to leave the house.

"Hello?" I said, knowing it was her.

"Hi Gina," she answered slowly. "Dad is gone."

"He is?"

"Yes. I was up with him all night and kept him
comfortable. His pulse kept getting weaker and weaker. About
fifteen minutes ago, he took one big breath, then another small
one, and that was it. I gave him some more morphine to make
sure he didn't feel any pain. He's gone. Hospice will be here
in an hour, and the funeral home will be here by 8:30."

I took a deep breath. "Okay. I just need to get dressed, and I'll be right over."

I walked into the bathroom where Doug was combing his hair. "My dad's gone, honey," I said. "I'm going over there now."

"Okay, do you want me to go with you?"

"It's totally up to you," I said.

"Yes, I'll call in." He gave me a big hug. "I'm so sorry," he said. I was reminded of having the same experience with his dad who died of cancer a year and a half before.

"I'm going to go wake up Mike now," I said. "We'll leave in about ten minutes okay?"

"Sure," he said.

I woke Mike up and delivered the news. "Oh Lord," he said, "peace at last."

"Are you going to be okay with seeing him dead?" I asked.

"Yes. It's just a shell that will be left. I'll be okay."

We went over to my mom's, and she greeted us at the door. "His pain is all gone," she said, with wet eyes.

Mike and I walked right in to look at my dad. I kneeled by his feet, and Mike rubbed his forehead. He suddenly looked very old. His eyes were black, his cheeks

were empty; he was nothing but grey skin and bones. Rigor
had already set in. His hands were clamped and blue.

I gently touched his feet, stared at him and cried. I
wanted to stay with him.

*I miss you, Dad. I hope you feel peace and comfort
now. I love you.*

I went up to his head and pulled the sheet lower so
that I could get a better look.

Yup, he's dead. He's gone.

I left the sheet down, but when my mom walked over
she covered his head with it.

Leave it down. I want to see him.

I bawled.

"Are you okay?" Mike asked.

"As strange as it is, I don't want him to go. I want him
to stay right here," I bawled. "I can't bear to say goodbye."

"It's not really him anymore, Gina. It's just his body,"
my mom said.

"I know. But I want to be with him."

*I bet Doug thinks I'm insane right now. I don't want
Dad to be gone.*

Doug came over and held me. We went over to the
couch and laid down together under the soft black blanket I
had bought dad when he was in the hospital.

"I love you," Doug said.

"Me too. Thank you."

For three hours, we sat in the living room, my dad dead on his hospice bed, Doug and I on the couch, Paul and Paula at the kitchen table, and Gabrielle and Derek helping my mom get things ready.

I can't believe he's really dead.

My aunt Paula came over and sat next to me on the couch, putting her hand on my arm.

She said, "You know, Gina, it has been so amazing seeing how your family has pulled together through this in such a loving way. The way you've been taking care of your dad and each other. This is the way it should be."

She continued, "My heart has been so heavy over the past few weeks. I work with a group of single moms in my church, and I've been mentoring a woman who is bi-polar, who was sexually abused by her step-father. She has two kids and is barely able to care for them let alone create a loving home."

What is she talking about? Did my mom tell her about me? I guess I don't care if she did. Does she know, or is this just a coincidence?

"The way that your family loves one another is so refreshing to see. It's been a real blessing," she added.

"Thank you," I said. "We're lucky." I cried.

Okay, that's enough. You can go sit back over there now. I can't take dealing with two issues at once.

8:30 a.m. came and went, and the funeral home team had not arrived yet. I thought about when Doug's dad died in the middle of the night, and the men showed up in suits. They had everyone say their final goodbyes and leave the room while they removed the body.

Finally shortly after 9:15 a.m., a black Suburban pulled into my parents' driveway. "The funeral home is here," I announced.

Two guys walked in the house, looking as though we had interrupted their hunting trip. One was in a camouflage jacket and hat with a RealTree logo on it. The other was wearing a jean jacket.

Oh my gosh. Who are these guys?!

"Please go ahead and take all of the sheets that he has on, and the pillows and everything," my mom said.

"Yes ma'am. No problem," said the first one.

The second one motioned that he was ready to slide my dad from his hospice bed onto the stretcher with the body bag.

Like pulling a deer out of the woods, they each grabbed an end and began to pull. I felt like I was watching a sick comedy.

Before I could, Mike rushed over to help them.

I can just see them dropping him on the floor now.

Once he was on the stretcher, the first guy began to zip him up in the bag. I could see my dad's hair still sticking out the top, and it looked as if his nose wasn't completely covered. I wanted to go fix it.

Just leave it. It doesn't matter. He's gone. It's just a dead body that they're going to cremate. It's going to get uglier from here. Just ignore them.

Mike was still right there with them, trying to help them toward the door.

"I want to stand up," my mom said. And, she stood up as if to salute my dad for one last time. I stood up with her. She covered her face with her hands and began to cry.

"Mike!" I shouted across the house. I waved for him to come over and support mom. He ran over. "Let's not watch," I said. And we hugged and held each other until they were gone.

That was gross and sad. And funny in a sick way. Who were those guys anyway?

I couldn't wait to get out of the house.

Knowing that my mom was in the capable hands of her sister and the rest of our relatives, I let her know that I was going home to get some rest. Doug, Mike and I left, and we assured her that we would be back later that day and that all she needed to do was call if she needed anything.

We spent the next three days planning the memorial service and reception. My mom wanted me to sing, and I agreed that I would try. Old school hymns. That's what he would want. Amazing Grace and How Great Thou Art. A Cappella.

Tuesday afternoon my aunt Marianne called me on my cell phone.

Good God, what would she be calling me for?

"Hi Gina, this is Auntie Marianne."

"Hello," I said, as warmly as I could given all of the circumstances.

"I'm so so sorry about your father," she said. "Auntie Ellen and I would like to come down for the funeral to be with your mum."

"Okay."

I really have no desire to see you, but you're my mom's sister, so I'll deal with it. As long as your asshole husband is nowhere around here. I know he's too chickensh*

to fly anyway, but you better not even be thinking about
bringing him.

"I understand that your dad's sister and her husband
are staying at your mum's, so would it be possible for Ellen
and I to stay at your house?"

"Sure," I said.

You know, it's fine, but holy crap. Again, if I was in
your shoes I wouldn't be calling me and asking favors let
alone – oh whatever!

"Okay, well, we'll see if we can get a flight, and I'll
let you know."

"Okay, that's fine," I said.

"All right. Thank you."

"Okay," I said and hung up.

"Mike!" I shouted upstairs.

"What?!"

"You're not going to believe this."

"What?"

"Auntie Marianne just called and asked if she could
stay here for the funeral!" I said.

"Oh Lord," he said. "Uncle Louis isn't coming, is
he?"

"No. She's planning on coming with Auntie Ellen."

"Oh phew. God, that's crazy."

"Can you believe it?"

"At least he's not coming."

"I'd take his ass out," Doug chimed in.

We all laughed.

On Thursday, we had the memorial service followed by a reception at mine and Doug's home. My Aunt Marianne supposedly ended up getting a really bad cold the day before, so she didn't come.

Thank God.

So many of my close friends were at the memorial – co-workers, family members, and friends of my parents. It was simple, peaceful and full of love just the way my dad would have liked it.

As prepared as I thought I was, I had not accepted my dad's death as well as I expected to. I cried and slept through most of the holidays, and I allowed myself to do that without feeling bad about it.

I skipped the McCabe family Christmas, and I didn't worry all day about what they were saying about me not being there.

I'm going to relax and take care of myself.

Cole called just as I was leaving my Pilates session.

"Heyyyy," I answered. *I'm so glad she called.*

"How are you?" she asked.

"I'm doing great. How about you?"

"Things are good, you know."

"Yeah?" I asked.

We spent some time catching up, talking about mutual friends, things that were going on in her life and mine. It took her a while to get around to saying what she really wanted to say.

"So I've been meaning to call you."

"Yeah?"

"I finally told my partner about the abuse."

"No way! You did? Good for you! I know how hesitant you were about that."

"Yeah. It's like the biggest weight is lifted off of my shoulders."

"Isn't it amazing?" I asked.

"It really is. And she was so great about it."

"Well of course she was. So, tell me, how did it go?" I asked gently.

"Well, first of all, I had to get half drunk just to admit anything. And as soon as I started explaining it I was crying my head off. But then it felt so good to just get it out there, you know? And she was so supportive, so nice about it all. It really brought us closer together, I think."

"I'm so proud of you, Cole. That was a huge step."

"I know. I feel so much better. I kept thinking about calling you."

"I'm glad you did! And now she can be supportive of you when you're going through the tough times, and you can tell her about your fears, the nightmares, the flashbacks – all of that crap. And she'll understand, and you won't feel so alone."

"Exactly."

We talked for a few minutes more, but I knew that's really all she wanted to tell me.

"I'll stop by and see you soon, okay?" I suggested.

"Yeah, do that," she said.

I'm so glad she told.

J anuary started off cold, but we didn't get the major storm that I had been hoping for. Big snow is one of the things I miss about Montreal.

Having been out of the office for the majority of December to deal with my dad's illness and death, I finally returned to work on the 2nd. I scheduled my first therapy session of 2008 two weeks later.

"Good to see you, Dr. Young," I said, as I walked into her office and sat down, feeling proud of myself for coming back.

"You too," she said. "I read your manuscript over the weekend."

"Oh, you did?" I asked.

"Yes," she said. "It gave me so much insight into everything you've been through – much more than I could ever get in our 50-minute therapy sessions."

"Great," I said.

I don't think she's ever seen me in a skirt before. I wonder if she thinks I look nice. I feel good in this. I kind of feel like I look pretty good, too. I wore pants to the eighth grade dance, to graduation, to parties and weddings and stuff. I didn't really like being too girly. When I wanted a truck, Dad asked why I always wanted to be so different. I remember when Dr. Young suggested that maybe the reason I became a firefighter was to assert my strength and reclaim the power that had been taken away from me. Hmm. I like being more like a girl now. I don't think I need to be afraid of that anymore.

"You've really been working on yourself, haven't you?"

"Yeah, I have," I said. "It's been good."

"Okay, one thing," she said with a smile on her face. "My chairs! You think they're gross and dirty?" she laughed. "I think they're quite clean."

I gasped a little, grinned and covered my mouth with my hand. I looked down. *Oops, I forgot I wrote that!*

"You're right. I don't know what to say except that when I came here the first day, that's how the chairs looked to me. Did you get new lighting in here or something? Everything seemed so dark and dingy before. Is that a new lamp?"

"Nope."

"Did you have the chairs cleaned?"

"No," she smiled.

"Huh." I inspected the chair I was sitting in, and I smiled. Not only was the blue fabric very clean, but the white piping along the edges was bright and perfect. "Well, I stand corrected."

"Anyway," she said, "it doesn't matter. I just thought I would ask."

"I take it back about the chairs," I said, and we both laughed.

"So did you read the part about me calling my uncle?" I asked.

"Yes, of course," she said, with a supportive look. "I was amazed at the courage it must have taken for you to do that."

"Believe me, I was shaking. And, you know, I think that the fact I was writing about it made me more able to do it. It was like, if I thought I needed to confront him, then I had to actually do it. And I wanted to do it so that I could write about it and tell others what it was like. I'm not sure that I would have ever gotten to it otherwise, although I really wanted to. The writing really helps for me. And, it felt great to confront him. It was almost as if I was able to confront him as an outsider, watching myself do it."

"And his reaction was so typical for an abuser," she said. "He was sort of all over the place and making excuses, unwilling to accept any blame, and so on."

"And how about my aunt?!" I asked. "She really pissed me off."

"Yes, I could tell," she smiled. "How she insisted on getting on the phone and so on."

"And then this crap that I wasn't going about healing the right way and that I just needed to forgive" I said. "I can't just expect to change everything about the way I think, feel, and act without really re-learning what normal is. I found that to be very judgmental."

"Do you think that your aunt uses that reasoning to validate why she stays with her husband?" she asked.

"I don't know," I said. "I didn't even think about that."

"Well, that's what I think," she said. "She's giving herself an excuse for staying with him. She has to forgive him to stay with him, and she's projecting those beliefs on you."

"Huh. Interesting," I said.

"So," she asked, "how would you like to start today?"

"Well, I'm looking forward to working through some more issues this year."

"Okay, like what?"

"Well, there's more to my story. I've come a long way, but there's more to tell and more work to do. I'm only comfortable opening up so much. I'm still learning how to open up – with your help, thank you. On one hand, I don't feel like it's necessary to tell every single detail. On the other hand, it's the undisclosed details that make me feel so awful. I try to make things sound better than they are, but I know deep down that I don't feel like everything is okay. I'm still afraid to admit a lot of things about the abuse, so I would like to work on that."

"Okay," she said, "that's – "

"Oh," I interrupted, "And I'm also leaving my job on January 25."

"You are?" she asked.

"Yes," I smiled. "I've been there since 2003, and as you know from our discussions over the past year, the company has been changing significantly. I love the people there, but I need to find something with a little less change going on – somewhere with more stability."

"Did you already give notice?" she asked.

"Yes. When I told the president that I wasn't going to stay, he asked if there was anything he could do to keep me, wished me the best, and told me I would always have a home there if I decided to come back. He couldn't have been nicer or more professional about it."

"That's great. So, what will you be doing next?"

I'm taking most of February off to finish the book and get it published, and then around the beginning of March, I'll start something new. Eventually, you know, I would like to open some sort of retreat center where people can come to unwind and do some self-exploration to work through hard times, like I've been through. Obviously, I can't just do that tomorrow, but I'm working on a transition plan so that I can do that eventually."

"Good for you," she said. "Have you found another job yet?"

"No," I smiled, "but I'm working on it. I've had several good discussions. I think I'll be able to lock something in by the end of the month. It will probably be something similar to what I've been doing, but at a company with a more established business and less overall volatility.

"Wow, you're going through a lot of change right now, aren't you?" she asked. "The book, your father's passing, a new job, all of this progress with yourself."

"Yes. A lot of change," I said. "I'm scheduled to go to an executive women's retreat in Connecticut at the end of January to envision what I want for 2008. I'm really excited. I'm going to try to figure out how I can start to integrate my desire to help other abuse survivors into my life this year."

"You've come full circle in some ways, haven't you?" she asked.

"I guess so," I said, with a smile. "Do you remember, during our first few months of therapy, you had suggested that I join a support group?"

"Yes," she said.

"And I was like 'No Way – not ready for that'?"

I was so scared.

"Yes, I remember."

"And you were suggesting that in order to heal, I would need to have some family and friends to support me, and I was like 'I'm not ready to tell.'?"

She nodded and smiled.

"And now, looking back, I've made so much progress. I still have a long way to go, but – just the fact that I told someone, right?"

"That's right," she said.

"It makes me feel so much better, so much safer," I said. "It's the years of secrets and the silence – that's what just tears you apart inside, isn't it?"

"It is."

"So how often do you think about the abuse now?" she asked.

"Uh. Well, I guess I think about it when I write about it or talk about it. And, I still have flashbacks sometimes at the beginning of intimacy with my husband, but not always. Other than that, I definitely don't think about it every day. Sometimes several days go by without it even crossing my mind. It's certainly not a hundred times a day like it used to be!"

"That's g – " she started.

I interrupted again, "Sorry. I can't believe I forgot to tell you. I've been surfing the web trying to find an organization that focuses on dealing with child sexual abuse in a real way, and I came across 'Stop the Silence'. Do you know about them?"

"No," she said.

"Well, stopping child sexual abuse is their mission. They work with schools, children, families, judges – they're creating awareness and delivering programs to prevent and treat child sexual abuse. Stop the Silence. It makes sense, right? Silence was such a big part of my problem! Anyway, I met with them, and we're working on finding a way to collaborate on our efforts this year. I'm so impressed with their work. And, you already know about the whole retreat thing that I eventually want to do – so, who knows, maybe the book will help make that happen. My mom and my brother want to work with Stop the Silence as well, so that will allow us to drive something positive together as a family."

"Now that Dr. Young was caught up with my progress, she wrapped up the discussion and closed our session. On the way out, I saw a young professional-looking man in the waiting room who looked like he didn't want to be noticed.

Remember how scared I was to come here? Remember being terrified of seeing someone I knew in the therapist's office? Remember how I thought the whole problem was my marriage?

He'll be okay.

As I got situated in the car, I stretched my thumbs, equally on both sides. I noticed I had been biting my teeth together frequently during the daytime again.

Try to relax. Be calm. Breathe.

I stretched my thumbs again. It hurt a little.

It's okay if you need to do that once in a while. It's okay. Don't fight it. Let it go.

Traffic on the Dulles Toll Road was heavy. Getting struck and killed right then crossed my mind, but only for a moment. The desire to end it all didn't linger this time. I was excited about my progress.

The more I let go of secrets, the more they lose their power. When I talk about the bad things, they don't seem so bad. They don't crush my spirit anymore. My life is becoming clearer every day.

What other people think of me is none of my business. When other people react negatively to me, it's about THEM, not me.

I called Doug to let him know that I was on the way home, and we talked about my therapy session.

THE BEGINNING

Where to go for HELP

*Child sexual abuse (CSA) is not one group's problem;
by expert accounts, it is a silent epidemic throughout the
world, creating social havoc – for the children, adult
survivors, and society. It can be prevented, and it can be
treated, but a conscious and sustained effort is both missing
and essential.*

Overview of
Stop the Silence: Stop Child Sexual Abuse, Inc.

Across the world, 150 million girls and 73 million
boys are subjected to forced sexual intercourse and other
forms of sexual violence (WHO, 2002). In the U.S. at least
one out of four girls and one out of seven boys are sexually
abused by 18 years old. Nearly 50 percent of all sexual
assaults are against girls aged 15 or younger. Outcomes often
include poor school performance, depression, psychosis,
promiscuity, teen pregnancy, prostitution, drug abuse, STIs
including HIV, homelessness, suicide and homicide, and
chronic disease.

The mission of *Stop the Silence* is to expose and stop CSA and help survivors heal worldwide. Our overarching goals are to: 1) help stop child sexual abuse (CSA) and related forms of violence; 2) promote healing of victims and survivors; and 3) celebrate the lives of those healed. Through our work, we aim to address the relationships between CSA and the broader issues of overall family and community violence, and violence within and between communities. Our focus underlines the importance of a shift in focus on positive development within our social complexes (e.g., the relationships between men, women, adults and children, cultural groups) to support peaceful – and to hinder violence-prone – relationships.

Support for services – In addition to having provided monetary and TA support to other groups providing direct service, *Stop the Silence* provides a virtual peer discussion group and is focusing on bringing more clinical services to a wider public.

Media Advocacy – a grant from the Department of Justice in 2005/2006 allowed *Stop the Silence* to broadcast public service announcements (PSA) in the U.S. and throughout the world. The International Race to *Stop the Silence*, held in various states and countries in collaboration with local groups, allows *Stop the Silence* and its collaborators to capture wide-based mass media attention. A global advocacy, education, and information program in collaboration with Durbin Institute of Technology and a technology firm, The Global Lesson Foundation, funded by these partners, is in process. Training for service providers – *Stop the Silence* staff and partners (Survivors Healing Center) have provided CSA and related training for the police in Zambia; in collaboration with the Cornell University, advocacy centers, various service groups, and with various Latino immigrant and others populations in California and elsewhere. The training has been shown to increase understanding of CSA and related issues.

Training for judges and other court-related personnel – Under DHHS, Ford Foundation, and DOJ awards, *Stop the Silence* has been providing local- and national-level information and training for judges and other court-related personnel. The training transcends legal systems.

Education and outreach – *Stop the Silence* reaches out to schools, day cares centers, houses of worship, etc. to catalyze a community response to prevention and healing. Also, an

HHS-supported colloquium, Stopping the Silence about Intimate Violence, with Naomi Nontombu Tutu and Riane Eisler, was held in 2005 with policy and NGO personnel to increase understanding.

From the standpoints of survivors, the non-abused public, or policymakers, CSA is wrapped in discomfort, shame, stigma, and fear. *Stop the Silence* focuses on CSA, as opposed to "child abuse and neglect" to bring it out of the shadows. The words "child sexual abuse," were consciously built into our name so that people learn to say them. We build awareness through training, education, policy development, and more.

Stop the Silence®
P.O. Box 127
Glenn Dale, MD 20769
301-464-4791
www.stopcsa.org

Pamela Pine, PhD, Founder and CEO
ppine@stopcsa.org

If you are a survivor of child sexual abuse or know of a child who has been abused or have other concerns, there are resources available. Go to **www.stopcsa.org** and click on the **Get Help** link.